# BOSTON
PUBLIC
LIBRARY

The Up-to-Date Biography of Henry Aaron: Quiet Superstar

About the Book

Curt Simmons, who tamed many batters in several big-league seasons, once said, "Henry Aaron is the only ballplayer I have ever seen who goes to sleep at the plate and wakes up only to swing as a pitch comes in." This book tells the fascinating story of Henry "Hank" Aaron waking up at the plate 715 times to beat Babe Ruth's home run record. The quiet, easy-going outfielder for the Braves, child of the Mobile black ghetto, attracted little attention for many years until he began to break batting records. Here is how quiet Hank ran gracefully to the Crown and became King Henry.

The Up-to-Date Biography of

Henry Aaron

Quiet Superstar

by **AL HIRSHBERG**

G. P. Putnam's Sons
New York

Copyright © 1969 by Al Hirshberg;
Copyright © 1974 by the Estate of Al Hirshberg

All rights reserved. Published simultaneously in
Canada by Longman Canada Limited, Toronto.

SBN: GB - 399-60915-6
SBN: TR- 399-20424-5

Library of Congress Catalog Card Number: 74-80656

PRINTED IN THE UNITED STATES OF AMERICA

10 up

Contents

1 Hero in Paradise 7
2 Boyhood of a Superstar 19
3 On the Way Up 31
4 Budding Star 45
5 Batting Champion 56
6 Most Valuable Player 71
7 Jaded Champions 88
8 So Near and Yet So Far 100
9 Steps Toward Immortality 116
10 Triple Crown Near Miss 126
11 Milwaukee Swan Song 138
12 The Atlanta Braves 153
13 Chieftain of the Braves 165
14 The Magic Number 178
Index 187

1 Hero in Paradise

While the ball sank into the Atlanta Braves' bullpen for his 715th home run, Henry Aaron circled the bases with his head bowed. Thousands rose from their seats to pay tribute on that night of April 8, 1974. Aaron's family and friends ran onto the field to praise and hug him for surpassing Babe Ruth's record 714. He had hit more home runs than any man in the history of professional baseball.

Seventeen years earlier, before an equally enthusiastic sell-out crowd of Braves fans in Milwaukee, Aaron crossed the plate for his forty-third time and first secured heroic stature in a tensely bristling game. On the night of September 23, 1957, the Braves played the St. Louis Cardinals, the only team standing in the way of their first pennant in Milwaukee.

The Braves were five games in front of the second-place Redbirds. Since both teams had six games to play, one Braves victory combined with one Cardinal defeat would clinch the pennant and transform Milwaukee from an ordinary American city into a madhouse. If the Braves won, it would be all over. If the Cardinals won, they would keep their chances alive and be a game closer to the top.

No fans in baseball history deserved a pennant more than Milwaukee's. They had embraced the Braves when the team arrived from Boston in 1953. They regarded the team as very special. Every man was a hero; every man could have whatever he asked for; every man had more favors, gifts, and jobs offered than he could handle. Color, race, creed meant nothing. Milwaukee had a baseball bender fever the likes of which the game had never seen before and probably never would again.

In the four years since the Braves had moved to Milwaukee from Boston they had finished second three times. Twice, in 1956 and 1955, they had been beaten out by the Brooklyn Dodgers. Loyal Milwaukee fans had suffered through both seasons hoping the big year had come. They were wrong both times.

But now the Dodgers were out of the race—embedded in third place. The 1956 and 1955 seasons were ancient history. This was 1957, the year of destiny in the eyes of every Braves follower in the land. Of course, all good baseball fans think the year of destiny is at hand before the season begins. Few have the satisfaction of seeing hope and promise as late as September 23. And for the Braves, there was more than hope and promise. With a five-game lead and only six to play, victory seemed around the corner.

As the confident Braves took the field for the game they expected would wrap up the pennant, they were greeted with roars from their frenetic fans. On the mound was Lew Burdette, the big right-hander from West Virginia. Del Crandall crouched behind the plate. At first base was huge Joe Adcock, at second the veteran switch-hitter Red Schoendienst, at short Johnny Logan, at third Eddie Mathews, well on his way to becoming one of the game's slugging immortals. In left field was Wes Covington, a rookie. In right field was the aging Andy Pafko.

And in center field was Henry "Hank" Aaron, second youngest batting champion in the history of the National League, perhaps baseball's best right-handed hitter since the peerless Rogers Hornsby (some observers liked him better than Willie Mays), possessor of the strongest, most resilient wrists the game has ever seen. Yet he was so self-effacing that hardly anyone seemed to know he was there.

He was tremendously fast, but not quite as fast as Mickey Mantle. He was a brilliant batter, but not quite as brilliant as Ted Williams. He was colorful in the sense that any great ballplayer, especially one who can hit with power to all fields and be a perpetual threat at the plate, is colorful, but nowhere nearly as colorful as Mays.

Even in 1957, Henry Aaron, at twenty-three a

fourth-year major-leaguer and a batting champion, was regarded as one of the great stars of his time—in fact, was taken for granted as one of the great stars of his time. And that was the key to the lack of attention given this sleepy-eyed young man from Mobile, Alabama. He was so good everyone took him for granted.

People took for granted his speed, his power, his consistency, his flawless fielding, his ability to diagnose a situation in an instant so that he always threw to the right base at the right time, and, most of all, his hitting.

For Aaron was the perfect hitter, as no one knew better than he himself.

"When I have my timing," he once said, "I can hit everyone. When I haven't, I can't hit anyone."

Although not overstating in the first instance, he was understating in the second. For even when his timing was off, Aaron could hit a baseball a mile. Often a bad-ball hitter, his wrists were so strong and elastic that he could wait until the last split second before whipping his bat around in a bewildering blur.

His teammate Warren Spahn, one of the great southpaw pitchers of all time, said of him, "It's fantastic how long he can look at a pitch before deciding to hit it."

Every catcher in the National League marveled at him. In different ways, they all said, in effect, "He takes the ball right out of your glove."

Charlie Dressen, who managed Aaron years later, called him "the best natural hitter I ever saw—better than Williams, better than Mays, better than DiMaggio, better than Musial, better than anyone."

When Aaron went to the plate, he stood deep in the batter's box, gently waving his bat, otherwise not moving a muscle. He stood straight, not crouched, and so still he seemed in another world. Although his eyes never left the pitcher, they were half-closed.

"Henry Aaron," said Curt Simmons, a great pitcher for the Phillies in the days Aaron first broke in, "is the only ballplayer I have ever seen who goes to sleep at the plate and wakes up only to swing as a pitch comes in."

Simmons, of course, was exaggerating outrageously, yet it was a fact that Aaron looked as though he were dozing while waiting for the pitcher to throw the ball. His trick of waiting until the last instant before lashing out with his bat intensified this illusion.

When he did lash out, his bat came around in a lightninglike arch, propelled by wrists so powerful they seemed to transform a 35-ounce bat into a toothpick. When he had his timing, he could, as he had said, hit anything anywhere, regardless of how baffling the pitch, regardless of whether it was in the strike zone or not.

Purists shuddered as they watched him swing, for Aaron broke one of the cardinal rules of batting. He hit off his front—his left—foot, something that no ordinary hitter could ever do successfully. Normally, this means the batter is shifting his weight instead of remaining in balance, thus cutting down his power.

But Aaron retained every bit of his power. In fact, his unorthodox style increased his power. And even when he was a rookie, no manager or coach dared correct him.

After watching him a few days, Charlie Grimm, who managed the Braves when Aaron first came to them in 1954, simply shrugged and said, "You'd be crazy to try to change a hitter like Henry."

Neither Grimm, nor Fred Haney, who succeeded him, nor any subsequent Braves managers ever attempted to correct Aaron.

Now, on this early autumn evening of 1957, Henry Aaron was one of many threats in the power-packed Braves' lineup. Every single man, even Burdette, was capable of driving the ball out of the park.

Schoendienst and Logan, the first two hitters, were the "table setters." Although both could hit home runs on occasion, their primary job was to get on base, "setting the table" for the power hitters who followed.

Mathews batted third and Aaron fourth. The day would come when these two would be hailed as the greatest one-two home-run punch in the history of baseball. By 1957 they were well on their way. Between them they were good for 76 home runs that year—44 for Aaron, 32 for Mathews.

Following Aaron came Adcock, third of the Braves' heavy-power men. The six-foot four-inch, 231-pound first baseman was nearly always good for at least 25 home runs a season; he probably would have been good for that number in 1957 except for a broken leg, which he had suffered in June. Now, back in the lineup just over two weeks and fully recovered, he was as great a threat as ever.

Next came Pafko, then Covington, then Crandall, and finally Burdette. None was a patsy for any pitcher.

Wilmer "Vinegar Bend" Mizell, a strong southpaw with an exploding fast ball and a tendency for wildness, was on the mound for St. Louis. When right, Mizell was hard to beat; when off his form, an easy man to get out of there.

Neither team scored in the first inning, and Burdette disposed of the Cardinals in the first of the second. When the Braves, who had gone down one, two, three in the first, came to bat in their half of the second, Henry Aaron was the lead-off man.

He belted Mizell's third pitch for a clean single to left, then went to second base on Adcock's hit. Pafko, ordered to bunt, did the job so well that he beat it out for a hit, filling the bases with nobody out for the Braves.

Covington hit an outfield fly, a ball which would score Aaron from third but figured to be an easy out. But Wally Moon, the Cardinals' center fielder, dropped it, leaving the bases still loaded with nobody out, one run in, and Del Crandall at bat.

With a right-handed hitter at the plate for the Braves, manager Fred Hutchinson of the Cardinals lumbered slowly out to the mound, took the ball away from Mizell, and waved Larry Jackson, a right-hander, into the ball game.

Jackson's job was to keep the Braves from hitting fly balls, and he did it perfectly. With the Cardinal infield in, Crandall grounded to third, forcing Adcock at the plate. When Burdette forced Pafko at home, the Braves threat was all but over. With the St. Louis infield back at normal depth, Schoendienst lined out to shortstop Alvin Dark to end the threat, and the inning ended with the Braves leading, 1–0.

Jackson was very tough from then on. While he held the Braves in check, the Cardinals caught and passed them with three key hits in their half of the sixth inning.

Wally Moon atoned for his error on Covington's fly in the second by reaching Burdette for a base hit. Then Stan Musial, one of baseball's superstars, belted a long fly into the hole in right center for a double, scoring Moon with the tying run. With two out, Dark punched a single to right, and Musial came home with the run that gave the Cardinals a 2–1 lead.

The top of the Braves' batting order tied it up again in the seventh. Schoendienst led off with a single and went to second on Logan's sacrifice bunt. Mathews brought Schoendienst home with a double to right for the first Braves run off Jackson.

Now it was 2–2, and it remained through the eighth and ninth, when Jackson went out for a pinch hitter. When the game moved into extra innings, the Cardinal pitcher was Billy Muffett, a rookie right-handed relief pitcher with a record of three victories and one defeat.

By this time the crowd was almost in hysterics. Every pitch, every swing, every time bat met ball, every play was greeted with roars. The game rocked on through a scoreless tenth inning; then Burdette, pitching brilliantly, blanked the Cardinals in the first half of the eleventh.

Muffett, who had set the Braves down in order in the tenth, faced Logan, the lead-off man in the last of the eleventh. The Milwaukee shortstop watched one pitch go by for a ball, fouled off the second, then hit the third on a line to center field for a single.

Eddie Mathews was up next. The powerful Braves third baseman belted a long fly to right center while Logan moved up the line between first base and second. Musial ranged back and over for the ball, caught it easily, and back to first scampered Logan.

Now, with one out, Henry Aaron stepped slowly to the plate. Just before he moved into the batter's box, he heaved a deep breath, exhaled, then took his stance. As Muffett peered in for the sign from his catcher, Aaron stood straight, his narrowed eyes staring under hooded lashes at the young Cardinal relief pitcher.

While Aaron wiggled his bat gently back and forth, Logan took a short lead. Muffet looked over at him once or twice but did not throw the ball to first. He went into his stretch, brought the ball down to his chest, took a last glance at Logan dancing off the bag, then threw toward the plate.

The crowd, stamping, clapping, yelling, was in an uproar, screaming at Aaron, screaming at Logan, screaming at Muffett, and the roar became almost a whine of anticipation as the ball left Muffett's hand.

Henry Aaron crouched ever so little, a sure sign that he was ready to swing. Waiting until the very last minute, he lowered his right shoulder, then whipped his bat around at a curve, almost picking the ball from the catcher's mitt.

Ball and bat met with a solid crash, and the crowd's whine became a wild, animal scream. The ball went toward center on a rising line, and a split second later it became obvious to the whole hysterical ball park that it wasn't coming down in center field.

Straight out it went, higher and higher, while Wally Moon, the Cardinals' center fielder, turned and ran to the deepest part of the ball park, where there was a sign marked 402 FEET. He leaped, but the ball was nowhere near his outstretched arm. It was gone, a home run, Henry Aaron's 43rd and next to last of the season.

Logan jumped high in the air as he ran around the bases ahead of Aaron. And Henry, normally phlegmatic, almost lost his cool. Grinning from ear to ear, he jumped up and down as he followed Logan on the base paths.

Later he told the press exactly what he was thinking.

"All I could think of was Bobby Thomson," he said. "I remember when he hit the home run that gave the Giants the nineteen fifty-one pennant. I remember that day so well. I stayed out of school to listen to the game on the radio. When Thomson came up in the ninth inning and hit one into the stands, I wondered what he was thinking as he ran around the bases."

Aaron looked around, grinned, and said, "Now I know."

The fans, of course, went crazy. Even while Aaron was circling the bases, strangers were pounding one another on the back, embracing, dancing up and down the aisles, and, if close enough to the field, spilling out to try to reach Aaron and his teammates.

Actually, the whole club, led by Logan, who **had**

scored ahead of him, was waiting for Aaron when he arrived at home plate. Still grinning broadly, Aaron practically floated into the arms of his mates. They raised him on their shoulders and rushed him to the dugout, the last of them barely beating the crowd, which was held back by ushers and police.

In the locker room, Henry, usually alone after every game unless he talked quietly to a reporter or two, was mobbed by writers, cameramen, television and radio people, and, of course, teammates.

Normally a shy, reserved man, he now just let himself go. As men came up to congratulate him singly and in groups, he kept repeating the same things over and over in answer to constantly repeated questions.

"Are you excited, Henry?"

"Boy, am I excited!"

"Were you ever as excited as this?"

"No, sir. This is the greatest thing that ever happened to me."

"Do you think this was your most important home run?"

"I don't just think so. I know it."

And over and over Aaron repeated his thoughts and feelings while running around the bases. It was almost as if Bobby Thomson, who actually had once been a teammate of Henry's at Milwaukee, were hovering in the background.

If anyone was happier than Aaron, it was manager Fred Haney. He had sweated out the whole season, wondering if this great ball club of his would really win. After the game the little Braves field boss walked around and around, shaking the hands of each of his men. And the heartiest handshakes of all were for Aaron.

In a masterpiece of understatement, Red Thisted of the Milwaukee *Sentinel* described in two sentences the effects of Aaron's home run.

"The Braves pennant became an accomplished fact at exactly 11:34 P.M. Monday night when Henry Aaron blasted a two-run homer for a 4–2 victory in 11 innings over the runner-up Cardinals," he wrote. "The 40,926 cash constituents at the stadium went slightly berserk."

If Aaron hadn't clinched the pennant for the Braves that night, somebody else perhaps might have. It didn't matter. What did was that Aaron was the hero, the man who gave the pennant to the Braves the way they wanted to win it—by beating their toughest competition and closest rivals in a head-to-head ball game.

It was hard to believe that the hero of this game, Milwaukees' man of the hour and hero of the season, was only twenty-three years old. This amazing young ballplayer had come a long way from his humble beginnings in the Deep South.

For only five years before, Henry Aaron, now world-famous, had been an absolute unknown everywhere except on the wrong side of the railroad tracks in Mobile, Alabama.

2 Boyhood of a Superstar

AFTER HENRY AARON reached the big leagues, he liked to tell baseball writers that he developed his marvelous wrist action by delivering ice as a kid in Mobile. Not until he had been in the majors for several years did he admit he could count the number of times he had delivered ice on the fingers of one hand.

"I don't know how I got these wrists," he said. "But it wasn't delivering ice."

Actually, the only jobs Aaron can remember as a kid were mowing lawns and, later, playing baseball. Second of the seven children of Herbert and Esteller Aaron, Henry was born in Down the Bay, a poor Negro part of Mobile, where his parents had moved from the farm town of Camden two years before.

His father soon was making a good enough living as a boilermaker's assistant at the Alabama Drydock and Shipbuilding Company to move to the much better neighborhood of Toulminville, and that was where Henry Aaron grew up. His three younger brothers were born there. One, Tommie, although nowhere nearly the ballplayer Henry is, eventually became one of his teammates with the Atlanta Braves.

The family lived in the frame house at 2010 Edwards Street which is still their home. Although his father wouldn't let Henry buy them a new house, he did accept his son's help in remodeling the old one. But anyone who remembers the place in the early forties when the Aarons first moved there, would recognize it today.

Henry fell in love with baseball as a kid, when he played anywhere, any time, and under any conditions. He first played for an organized team when he caught for Toulminville Grammar School in the Louisiana Recreational League, a Negro softball loop in Mobile. Actually, it was years before Aaron played anything but softball.

His unorthodox habit of batting off his left foot today was conventional compared to the way he batted as a youngster. In those days he batted cross-handed; in other words, as a right-handed hitter, he stood at the plate with his left hand gripping the bat above his wrist. Besides being an invitation for a broken wrist, this cuts power down to a minimum.

"I probably should have become a switch-hitter," Aaron says. "It would have been easy for me to move to the other side of the plate, where the left hand does belong over the right. Instead, I learned to hold the bat properly while remaining a right-handed batter. Believe me, it wasn't easy."

The reason it wasn't easy was that Aaron batted cross-handed right up to the time he turned professional—all through grammar school and high school. Yet he hit the ball hard enough to pile up astronomic batting averages. One year he was over .700.

Next to playing ball, his favorite pastime was sitting in the bleachers at Mobile's Hartwell Field watching barnstorming big-leaguers in action. In those days, all major-league clubs went North from spring training by rail instead of by air, and Mobile was a regular stop. At one time or another, Henry saw practically every major-league club that trained in Florida.

His first hero was Joe DiMaggio; his second, Jackie Robinson; his last and permanent idol, Stan Musial. When Aaron, born in 1934, was eight, he saw the Yankees—and DiMaggio—for the first time. After World War II, when he was twelve and DiMaggio was back in baseball from Army service, Henry saw DiMaggio play in Mobile again. In the meantime, he read everything he could find about the great Yankee star. To this day, Aaron worships DiMaggio from a distance. He has been introduced to DiMaggio a few times but has never talked at length with him.

Aaron's affinity for Jackie Robinson, who broke baseball's color line when he entered the Brooklyn Dodgers organization in 1946, was natural. But although he later played against Robinson and got to know him rather well, Aaron was never close to Robinson. The man he admired most—as he still does—was Stan Musial. The reason, in all probability, was that Musial was precisely the kind of ballplayer Aaron hoped someday to become. And oddly enough, although Aaron wasn't aware of it at the time, Musial was—and is—much the same kind of person.

Both men were quiet, self-effacing, and modest, and both had to be drawn out before they would talk much to strangers. Both had a tendency to pooh-pooh their own accomplishments, to call everything they did simply part of a day's work. And both were easily overlooked in crowds because of their reluctance to be the center of attention.

There was the same similarity between them as hitters. Neither deliberately went for home runs, yet both hit many more than their share. Both had marvelous wrists that enabled them to wait on every pitch until the last split second before deciding whether to swing or not. And both ranked high among the most valuable ballplayers who ever lived.

No doubt, as every kid does, Henry Aaron devised imaginary conversations with Musial. Later, when he himself became a big-leaguer, he used to tell newspapermen how much Musial helped him and to give Musial credit for his own outstanding stretches at the plate. Stories of this nature often appeared on sports pages until Musial himself was once asked about them.

"Henry Aaron is a marvelous ballplayer," Musial replied. "And everything he has done he did himself. He certainly never got any help from me. The only words we have ever exchanged were 'Hello,' 'How are ya?' and things like that. He never asked me for advice and I never gave him any."

Whether these "talks" with Musial were a carry-over from childhood fantasy or Aaron's way of gently kidding the press will probably never be known. But Henry's earliest days as a big-leaguer were close enough in years to his days as a hero-worshiping young fan to make it appear that his imaginary conversations with Musial were still fresh in his mind when he finally played against the Cardinals' star.

Modesty or no modesty, Henry certainly didn't lack confidence in himself. Whenever he came home from watching an exhibition game at Hartwell Field, he told his mother, "Someday I'll be out there. Someday I'll make the big leagues."

She probably didn't know what the big leagues were.

Her one burning ambition for Henry and her other children was for them to acquire an education.

When he was fourteen and had become one of the outstanding softball players in Mobile, Henry told his close friend Connie Gilles, "I'm a good ballplayer. I know I am. I'll make it. I'll make it all the way to the top."

Gilles knew exactly what Henry was talking about. And he knew Henry well enough to believe his friend *would* make it when he grew up.

After Toulminville Grammar School, Henry caught and played short and third for Central High. Still batting cross-handed, still playing mostly softball, he was far and away the outstanding baseball player in school. The team, coached by Edwin Foster, won the Negro high school championship of Mobile two years in a row, losing only three games.

Although he weighed only 150 pounds, Henry also played football at Central, where he made the all-city team as a guard. But because he preferred baseball and didn't want to spoil his future with a football injury, he gave the game up after a year.

After he had spent two years at Central High, Henry's parents sent him to Josephine Allen Institute, a private secondary school in Mobile. By this time he was determined to become a professional ballplayer, but neither of his parents approved. They wanted him to finish high school and then go on to college.

He was already making money—not much, but a little—from baseball. As a shortstop and third baseman with the Pritchett Athletics, he collected $3 a game, playing mostly on Sundays. The Athletics were his first hardball team, but that didn't matter. He could still murder the ball, was nearly always on base, starred in the field, and showed more promise than any ballplayer in Mobile. At fifteen he was signed by the Mobile Black Bears, the fastest semipro team in town. It played a couple of twilight games a week, and Billy Tucker, the owner, paid Aaron $3 to $5 a game, depending more on how much money he collected from the crowd than on how well Henry did.

Henry's lack of aggressiveness cost him a possible chance to get into the Dodgers organization when he went to a Brooklyn tryout camp in Mobile at the age of fifteen. He stood around with his glove in his hand waiting for a chance to go on at shortstop, but when he made his move, a bigger boy pushed him aside. The same thing happened when he tried to approach the plate to hit.

Disgusted and upset, he left the tryout camp without doing anything. It was a blow at the time, for, in common with many youthful Negro ballplayers, he preferred the Dodgers, the club which had opened the way for all Negroes by signing Robinson.

Henry got his first big break in the late summer of 1951, when the Indianapolis Clowns of the Negro American League came to Mobile for a game against the Black Bears. Although the league was faltering—its best players were going into the majors—the Clowns, still a good ball club, had not stopped looking for talented young prospects.

Playing against a team far better than his own, Aaron collected two singles and a double and starred in the field. Clowns' players and executives alike, deeply impressed with the seventeen-year-old youth, were amazed at his all-around skill.

But Syd Pollock, the owner, was more amazed that he could do so well batting cross-handed.

"I want that boy," he said. "But the first thing we must do is teach him to hold the bat properly. I never saw anyone hit the ball so hard cross-handed."

After the game, Bunny Downs, the Clowns' road secretary, said to Aaron, "How would you like two hundred dollars a month to play for us?"

"I'd like it," Henry said, "but I doubt if my mother would. She wants me to go to college."

Mrs. Aaron had already decided to send Henry to Florida A and M in Tallahassee, and this meant he would have to finish high school. When he told her he wanted to join the Clowns, she flatly refused to let him. They finally compromised. Henry could sign with the Clowns without going to college, but he would first get his high school diploma.

The following season the Clowns' contract arrived

with instructions for Henry to report to them at Winston-Salem, North Carolina, for spring training. His rail ticket was enclosed. Henry celebrated by buying a sports jacket to go with his two pairs of trousers, then packed his belongings in an old suitcase. Armed with sandwiches made by his mother and accompanied by the whole family, he went to the railroad station. After tearful farewells and promises to write, he was off on the first leg of his professional baseball career. It was the first time in his life he had ever been away from home.

Even with a contract, trying to work out with the Clowns was nearly as hard as at the Dodgers' tryout camp. The Clowns' camp was so jammed that Henry couldn't even get a warm-up jacket. He stood around shivering for half an hour before he managed to get into the batting cage for a few swings. He was chased out after hitting two balls on a line.

Later during Aaron's first day in camp, Dewey Griggs, a Braves' scout who had heard about Henry, watched him warming up, then said, "One thing bothers me. You throw everything underhand. Can't you throw overhand?"

"Sure," Henry said. "But I'm freezing. I don't have a warm-up jacket and I don't want to strain my arm."

Griggs turned and roared to the trainer, "Get this kid a warm-up jacket!"

A warm-up jacket was finally produced, and Aaron began to have an easier time. Pollock, who took a deep interest in him, insisted that he have as much time as he wanted in the batting cage, and soon Henry was installed as the club's regular shortstop.

Right from the start the Clowns worked on breaking Aaron of his distressing habit of batting cross-handed. And right from the start Henry, without really meaning to, resisted. He knew he would never go farther in baseball until he learned to hold the bat properly. But this meant changing what he had been doing all his life, and that wasn't easy. For the first few weeks he was with the Clowns he had to be constantly corrected.

"Even after I broke the habit," he said later, "I sometimes slipped right back into it. If there were two strikes on me and my back was to the Clowns' dugout so they couldn't see me, I would sneak the left hand up top because it was more comfortable."

Wherever he went, he hit the ball hard, and soon Dewey Griggs wasn't the only big-league scout watching him. The Giants, the Yankees, and the Phillies all were after him before the Negro American League season was two weeks old.

The Clowns played day and night, two, sometimes three games at a time. The schedule was haphazard, made up week by week, with frequent last-minute changes. Travel was by bus, and accommodations were whatever the ball club could get. Only in the big leagues could Negro ballplayers get into first-class hotels, and most good restaurants were also closed to them at the time.

On the first and fifteenth of every month Aaron got a check for $100. He sent all but $25 a month to his mother, for his own needs were minimal. His living expenses were paid, he neither smoked nor drank, and he wasn't fussy about clothes. Often he didn't even spend the little money he kept for himself.

His greatest luxury was sleeping, and soon he was famous all over the league as being the sleepingest ballplayer in history. He could sleep anywhere, any time, under any conditions—on buses, in locker rooms, anywhere. He could doze off for five minutes or sleep for five hours, and that was over and above the sleeping he did in bed at night.

He couldn't always go to bed. Sometimes the Clowns had such long jumps—such as from Kansas City to Buffalo, for example—that they spent two days and two nights on the bus, stopping only to stretch or eat. While his teammates killed the long hours reading, playing cards, or talking, Henry slept. Often, from the beginning of a trip to the end, he wasn't awake for more than an hour.

He never hurried, yet was never late. He took his time even in ball games. Griggs, noticing that Aaron, after fielding a ball, waited until the last minute before throwing it to first, asked Henry why he didn't move faster.

"When I was a little kid," Aaron replied, "my daddy told me never to hurry unless I had to. I never forgot that."

He didn't talk much about it at the time, but when he played for the Clowns, Henry had four ambitions, all of which he eventually realized. One was to play in the big leagues. Another was to win the Most Valuable Player award. The third was to win a batting championship. And the fourth was to play in the World Series.

As Aaron tore the Negro American League apart with his bat, there was little question that he was on his way. He had some amazing days and nights that contributed to his tremendous batting average. He hit a home run his first time at bat in a regular league game, then followed with a single and two doubles. From then on, he never went a day without at least one hit.

His greatest performance came in a doubleheader against the Kansas City Monarchs at Buffalo. The club played a single game in Washington, then traveled all night and all the next day in the bus. Everyone else was dead tired when the boys arrived in Buffalo, but not Henry, who had slept a solid twenty-four hours.

In the first game he had a home run, two doubles, and a single. In the second, an extra-inning affair, he collected 6 more hits, for a total of 10 hits in eleven times up. He also started five double plays, stole a couple of bases, drove in almost all of the Clowns' runs, and lifted his batting average to .467.

That did it. The major-league scouts who had been following him, went right to work, not on him but on Syd Pollock. Pollock, partial to the Braves, had already written John Mullen, their farm director, inviting an offer for Henry. Mullen authorized Dewey Griggs to go as high as necessary to get him.

This, of course, was at a time when big bonuses were still unheard of. Besides, Henry, as the property of the Clowns, would get no slice of the purchase price. However, he could control his salary. He didn't have to go anywhere he didn't want to.

Pedro Zorilla, a Puerto Rican scout employed by

the New York Giants, offered Aaron a Class A contract at $250 a month.

"They're pikers," Griggs told the youngster. "The Braves will pay you three hundred and fifty and send you to a Class C club, where you won't have so much pressure."

Both the Braves and the Giants offered Pollock about the same—somewhere in the neighborhood of $10,000—for Aaron. Pollock gave the kid his choice.

"What do you think I should do?" Henry asked.

"I'd take the Braves," Pollack said. "The Giants are offering a Class C salary to play Class A ball."

It wasn't until later that Aaron learned Pollock had nearly closed a deal with the Giants, who were so sure they had Henry they were astounded when he went to the Braves.

Manager Leo Durocher of the Giants was more than just astounded. He was absolutely furious.

"How could we have lost that boy?" he demanded. "We could have had him any number of times. Why, one of our scouts umpired a high school game he played in and never told us a word about him. And if what we offered him wasn't enough to satisfy him, why didn't we go higher?"

Durocher already had Willie Mays, who joined the Giants in 1951. Fans of the Giants, who moved to San Francisco in 1957, have been almost as upset as Durocher was. With a one-two punch of Mays and Aaron, they said, who could tell how many pennants the Giants might have won when the two stars were in their prime?

3 On the Way Up

THE BRAVES, in accordance with a system often used by big-league clubs when they bought a player from a team not in organized baseball, had an escape clause in their agreement to purchase Aaron. They gave the Clowns a down payment of $2,500, with the rest to be paid after thirty days if they were satisfied with Aaron. If they weren't, they could return him to the Clowns, who would keep the down payment, and the deal would be off.

The Braves assigned Aaron to their farm club at Eau Claire, Wisconsin, in the Class C Northern League. The club, managed by Bill Adair, a grizzled veteran of many minor and a few major-league campaigns, was so desperate for a shortstop that Aaron was flown up from Charlotte, North Carolina, where the Clowns happened to be the day he was sold.

For anyone else, it would have been a routine flight, but Henry had never flown before. Frightened to death before he got on the plane, sick to his stomach almost from takeoff, he was a nervous and physical wreck when he arrived in Eau Claire—just in time to dress for a ball game.

One minute he thought he was going to die. The next he was out on the ball field, cured of all his ailments. For, as always, it looked like any other ball field to Henry, and he picked up at Eau Claire just where he had left off with the Clowns. He got two hits in his first game, one in his second, and it wasn't long before he was recognized as the most dangerous batter in the league.

Although not a great shortstop, he was good enough, and he continued to hit Northern League pitchers as if he owned them. After only two weeks he made the league all-star team, and by the end of his thirty-day trial period there was no question about the Braves' keeping him. They sent the Clowns the balance of the $10,000 purchase price, and Henry was on his way.

Pitchers who had faced him were scared to death of him, and pitchers who hadn't were in no hurry to do so. He drove everyone crazy because he seemed to have no weakness at the plate. One day manager Charlie Fox of St. Cloud ordered his hurler to brush Aaron back. When a fast ball came in less than two inches from Henry's nose and he hammered it on a line to left-center field for a double, Fox threw up his hands and muttered, "I give up."

Everybody gave up. Aaron hit bad pitches as hard as good ones, close pitches as far as outside pitches, curves as solidly as fast balls. When opposing pitchers met to gossip about the league's hitters, Henry was always a prime subject.

"How do you pitch him?" one would say.

And another would shrug and reply, "There's no way to pitch him."

One thing they all agreed on. It was suicide to pitch Aaron tight. Rather than go down to avoid a close pitch, he simply fell away and creamed it.

"Last time I threw one at his head," one pitcher confided to another, "he hit it out of the park. There's just no point in trying to dust him off."

Although Aaron didn't hit many home runs—he had nine during that 1952 season—most of those he did hit were tape-measure jobs. Both teammates and opponents marveled at his power. At eighteen Aaron had not yet reached his full growth of six feet or his full weight of 175 pounds, and he looked almost frail as he stood at the plate. But with those wrists flicking at precisely the right moment, he could hit a ball tremendous distances and with the velocity of a rifle-shot.

A typical Aaron hit started on a low line, rose as it gathered speed, and came down like a bullet. Even outfielders camped under one of his murderous line drives found it difficult to hold them. During the last two-thirds of the season—which was all Aaron played because he reported to Eau Claire in May—he must have reached base twenty times on outfield errors when fielders couldn't make plays on line drives right into their hands.

Aaron's inexperience was all that kept him out of the majors then and there. He made mistakes in the field which cost ball games. Great as he was at the plate, he needed help in diagnosing pitches. He still seemed awkward at times because, although he no longer batted cross-handed, he wasn't yet used to holding the bat properly.

And he was still a kid, both in appearance and in action. He lived at the YMCA in Eau Claire, a lonely, unhappy youth so homesick that there were times his mates thought he would take off for Mobile any day.

Although people did as much as they could to make him feel at home, Aaron was sensitive to the fact that he was black in what was then nearly an all-white world. In Mobile there had been places he could not go, doors he could not enter, bus seats he could not sit in. These were familiar restrictions which did not exist in Eau Claire, and he couldn't get used to what was, for him, a new kind of freedom.

Nor did he find it easy to fraternize with teammates of another race. All the Clowns were Negroes. When they traveled in the South, they all were in the same boat. What was closed to one was closed to all. Aaron, who could not even have got into a YMCA in the South, still missed the companionship of his own people.

Both on and off the field, he was a clam, speaking only when spoken to and even then talking as little as possible. His love for sleep was as great as ever. He dropped off wherever he was, sometimes snoozing right in the locker room.

Adair wasn't quite sure what to make of him. Asked for an evaluation of him from the Braves, he replied, "No one can guess his IQ because he gives you nothing to go on. He sleeps too much and looks lazy, but he isn't. Not a major-league shortstop yet, but as a hitter he has everything in this world."

Billy Southworth, a former Braves' manager who did special scouting jobs for the ball club, once went to Eau Claire to watch Aaron in a three-game series. He sent general manager John Quinn a long report on the youth. It read in part:

"Aaron has all the qualifications of a major league shortstop and he runs better than average.

"On the latest official Northern League batting averages, Aaron is hitting .345. He is a line-drive hitter, although he has hit a couple of balls out of the park for home runs. He has quick hands, gets the ball away fast and accurately. He gets a good jump on the ball and can range far to right or left. I saw him go deep in the hole to his right and field a slow-hit ball. He came up throwing and virtually shot his man out going to first base. This was a big league play in my book because I did not think he had a chance to retire the man. He has a strong arm.

"Aaron started two double plays and completed one from the pivot position. He threw sidearm, not overhand. His arm is strong and he does not have to straighten up to throw.

"Aaron turned 18 last February. Consequently, I like his chances of becoming a major league player far more than either Gene Baker of Los Angeles or James Pendleton of Montreal, first because of their ages, then, too, because I think Aaron has better hands than either of the others. He has proven his ability in the short time he has been here.

"Baker and Pendleton are faster, but this boy will outplay them in all departments of the game when he has more experience.

"Second game I watched him play—on Aaron's first trip to the plate he hit a home run over the left-center fence. He collected three hits for the evening and had three runs batted in. He had four chances with one error. Oh, yes, he also had a stolen base. For a baby-faced kid of 18, his playing ability is outstanding.

"I will see one more game tonight but will send in this report now, because whatever happens tonight will not change my mind in the least about this boy's ability."

Although both Baker and Pendleton also made it to the majors, Southworth was right in his comparison of Aaron to them. Baker went to the Cubs, where he played second base for several years, but not nearly as long as Aaron stayed up. And Pendleton, originally the property of the Dodgers, eventually was sold to the Braves, where he was a teammate of Aaron's for only a few years before fading into obscurity.

Aaron, after playing only 87 games for Eau Claire to finish the 1952 season, was a unanimous choice as the Northern League's rookie of the year. He batted .336, scored 89 runs, had 116 hits, and drove in 61 runs. Although he didn't lead the league in anything, he probably would have led it in everything if he had played the entire season.

Despite his great season at Eau Claire, he didn't go much higher in 1953. The Braves, hesitant to move a nineteen-year-old up too fast and loaded with top talent at Milwaukee, promoted him only to the Jacksonville Tars in the Class A South Atlantic League. Popularly known as the Sally League, this Southern stronghold of the minors had never before had a Negro ballplayer. Aaron was one of three to break the color line there. Fortunately for him one of the other two was Felix Mantilla, a Jacksonville teammate.

Later a Braves official said, "We would not have sent Aaron to the Tars without Mantilla. He had pressure enough without carrying any extra burdens."

Actually, there were plenty of extra burdens anyhow, but Aaron, being a Southerner, knew what to expect—and got it. As the club traveled about the circuit by bus, he and Mantilla had to sleep elsewhere while their mates lived in hotels. When they stopped on the road to eat, they had to wait in the bus for someone to bring them food because they weren't allowed in any of the roadside cafés. And wherever they went, they were subject to the Jim Crow laws then in effect.

But all of Aaron's discomforts were off the field. On it he was happy. His salary was raised to $400 a month, and he was worth three times as much. Sensational as ever at the plate, he never failed to amaze Ben Geraghty, his manager. Nor, for that matter, did Geraghty ever fail to amaze him.

Later he said, "Geraghty was the kindest, most understanding manager I ever had. And he was a fine baseball man who knew the game as well as anyone."

Aaron's memories of Geraghty were so warm that he resented the Braves' refusal to promote his old Jacksonville manager to the big club. After Fred

Haney retired in 1959, to be succeeded by Charlie Dressen, Aaron said, "I have nothing against Dressen, but they should have given Geraghty the job."

While handling Aaron well, Geraghty certainly didn't coddle him. When Henry made a mistake, he heard about it. The manager never hesitated to let him know when he was careless, or missed a signal, or did things that got the ball club into trouble during games.

One day at Jacksonville, Henry stole second, then wandered off the bag before the second baseman tossed the ball to the pitcher and was tagged out. As he trotted back to the dugout, Geraghty gave him a dirty look, so he quickly turned his head away.

The next time up, after singling, he stole second again. Once more he dusted himself off, then took a step off the bag too soon and was tagged. That time he didn't even look in Geraghty's direction when he returned to the bench.

After reaching first his third time up, Henry stole second for the third time. He slid into the bag, jumped up, then, without asking for time out, moved off again. And for the third time he was picked off.

In the eighth inning it happened again. Henry reached, stole, stepped off the bag, and was nailed. That time Geraghty didn't let him stay out of the way.

"Once," the manager said, "I can forgive. Twice is pretty bad. Three times is gross carelessness. And four is ridiculous."

Henry apologized and promised to be more careful in the future. Oddly enough, he was. He never again got caught off base by a fielder holding the ball after he had stolen.

In telling of the incident later, Aaron said, "One wonderful thing about Geraghty was that he never made us feel worse than we did already by bawling us out after we lost. It was only after we won that we heard from him. And that day I got caught four times, we won. Mad as he was, he wouldn't have said a word to me if we had lost."

Aaron, like Yogi Berra, hated signs, partly because he didn't need them, but mostly because he couldn't remember them. He was especially bothered when signs were changed, as they sometimes had to be.

One day, after Geraghty had produced a new set of signs, he gave Henry the sign to take the next pitch, to let it go by. But it came right through the slot, and Aaron belted it over the left-field fence. After he had rounded the bases, Geraghty said, "Why didn't you take the pitch when I signaled?"

"I thought that was the hit sign," Aaron said.

"That was the old hit sign," Geraghty said.

"Gee, Ben," Aaron said, "I just learned that one yesterday."

Sometimes—probably such as then—Geraghty didn't know how to take the youth.

"I never knew when he was pulling my leg," Geraghty once said. "He's got that deadpan look on his face. Lots of times you thought he was serious when he was kidding."

Sportswriters, frequent victims of Aaron's gentle humor, weren't sure how to take him either. It was at Jacksonville that he first gave out the story about having developed his wrists hauling ice. After that had been played up in the sports pages, Aaron quite seriously told a writer that the only job he had ever had in Mobile was mowing lawns. He told one writer that he liked to hunt in winter, another that he never hunted because it was too dangerous.

He mystified even his teammates by his utter indifference to the identity of opposing pitchers. Whenever there was a discussion on the bench about the other pitchers, Aaron sat quietly, apparently half dozing in a corner of the dugout.

One of his Jacksonville teammates later said, "He almost convinced us he didn't know one pitcher from another, but he must have. Whenever a pitcher handcuffed him one night, Henry murdered the guy the next time he faced him. You don't do that not knowing who he is or what to expect from him."

Aaron had the same apparent indifference to the kind of bat he used. He never went to the bat rack to pick and choose; he simply grabbed the first bat he got his hands on and took it up to the plate with him.

One day during spring training, he hit a home run off Gene Conley in an exhibition game against Toledo, the Braves' top farm club. As Henry was trotting to the Jacksonville bench after circling the bases, the next hitter asked, "Which bat did you use?"

"The Greenberg model," Aaron said.

"You couldn't have," the other player said. "I've got that one."

"Well," Aaron said, "it was some bat. It must have been the right one."

Since Mantilla was the shortstop, Aaron shifted to second base the year he played for the Tars. He was neither better nor worse there than he had been at short. Hardly a stick-out, he and Mantilla were last in the league in double plays. Yet opinions about his play in the field conflicted.

One Braves' scout, after watching him for several days, sent back word that Aaron "is a big-league hitter right now. But his fielding is very doubtful."

Yet Oscar Roettger, a farmer major-league second baseman who lived in Jacksonville, announced, "Milwaukee has a dandy in Aaron. I saw him several times and I didn't see him do anything wrong. He made all the plays, and rather easily."

And Gabe Paul, then general manager of the Cincinnati Reds, told observers, "Our scouting reports say he is good enough defensively to hang on in the majors."

Good, bad, or indifferent in the field, Aaron was hitter enough to lead Jacksonville to the Sally League pennant that year. He started slugging on opening day and never stopped. He rattled a double off the left-field wall to score a run off Corky Valentine of Columbia his first time up, then saved the game in the ninth with another double.

Later in the season, with the pennant riding on a pair of doubleheaders against Columbia, Aaron went wild. The first day he had 7 hits in 8 times up in the two games. The second day he collected 5 hits and walked 3 times for a total hit production in the series of 12 for 13. Jacksonville swept all four games and clinched the pennant. It was the Tars' first flag in forty-one years.

When the season was all over, Geraghty said, "If Henry has a strike zone, it's from the top of his head to his ankles. In a year or so he'll make the fans forget Jackie Robinson, and I'm not exaggerating. He never pays any attention to who's pitching. He hits them all."

Aaron was the Sally League's top man in nearly everything. He won the batting championship with a .362 average. He led in runs batted in with 125, in runs scored with 115, in hits with 208, in total bases with 338, and in doubles with 36. He was second in home runs with 22 and second in triples with 14. And with three-quarters of the writers, some of whom had openly disapproved the league's breaking the color line, voting for him, he easily won the Most Valuable Player award.

"Henry Aaron," said one writer, "led the league in everything but hotel accommodations."

Aaron has warm memories of Jacksonville, for besides gaining the stature of a budding superstar there, he met and married his wife there. Shortly after opening day, standing on the street in front of his roominghouse, he saw a pretty girl walking into the post office. Henry hurried into the house for T. C. Marlin, the Tars' clubhouse steward, who knew everyone in Jacksonville.

When the girl came out of the post office, Aaron pointed and said, "If you know her, introduce me as the next great coming hitter of baseball."

"I know her," Marlin said. "She's Barbara Lucas. She's taking courses at Walker's Business College."

When Marlin introduced Henry to her, she said, "I was at the game last night. I saw you play."

After an awkward silence, since Henry hadn't had

On the Way Up

a hit in five times up the night before, he said, "You come out again tonight and I'll hit a few in your honor."

And that night, with Barbara in the stands again, he had a single, a double, and a home run.

He took her out all summer but her parents were not enthusiastic about her going with a ballplayer. One night her father said, "What other work have you done?"

"Well," said Henry, "I was once in agriculture."

"Doing what?"

"Picking strawberries," he replied.

In the midst of a civic dinner in honor of the ball club, Aaron suddenly got up from the head table, hurried to a telephone, and called Barbara.

"I want you to marry me right away," he said. "Can I have your answer now, please?"

"My answer is yes," she said. "But only if my father approves."

"Put him on," Henry said.

Then, with cheers for him and his teammates in the background, he sold himself to Barbara's father over the phone. He and Barbara were married on October 6, and she went with him to Caguas, where he played in the winter Puerto Rican League.

Felix Mantilla was on the team, and so were several big-league ballplayers, including Jim Rivera, Ruben Gomez, Luis Arroyo, Charlie Neal, Brooks Lawrence, and Vic Power. The manager was Mickey Owen, a good hitting teacher, although not an outstanding hitter himself.

Owen had two important tips to contribute to the

making of a superstar. First, he got Aaron to crouch so that he could hit to the opposite field. Henry had been standing up straight and hitting almost everything to center and left. Second, Owen got him to learn the strike zone, even if he ignored it when hitting bad balls.

At the request of the Braves, Owen played Aaron in the outfield. It was the first time since he had joined the organization that Henry played anywhere but short or second.

He did not become a finished outfielder in Puerto Rico. But he looked promising enough for Owen to report back to the Braves that he was ready for the majors.

The Braves weren't so sure. They put him on the Toledo roster but told him to report to the major-league spring training camp at Bradenton, Florida, in the spring of 1954.

For the ball club, it was no more than a gesture. For Henry Aaron, it was the chance of a lifetime.

4 Budding Star

WHEN AARON reported for spring training in 1954, the Braves, who had finished second the year before, had a set lineup. Joe Adcock was at first, Danny O'Connell at second, Johnny Logan at short, Eddie Mathews at third, Andy Pafko, Bill Bruton, and Bobby Thomson in the outfield, Del Crandall behind the plate, and a great pitching staff was spearheaded by Warren Spahn and Lew Burdette.

"Where do you put Aaron?" somebody asked manager Charlie Grimm one day.

"I can't imagine," Grimm replied. "He's a fine young prospect, but we just don't seem to have room for him."

"Will you keep him?"

"If he doesn't break into the regular lineup—and I don't see how he can—I wouldn't recommend it," Grimm said. "He's on the Toledo roster. It would be better for him to play there every day than sit on the bench up here."

The question of Aaron's making it at short or second was never considered. Logan was one of the better shortstops in the league. O'Connell, acquired from the Pittsburgh Pirates for a big price, was expected to be the Braves' second baseman for years.

Henry was considered an outfielder, but in the early days of spring training in 1954, he seemed completely shut out there, too. Pafko, the right fielder, was getting along in years, but he still had several good seasons left. Bruton, one of the fastest men in the majors, had a lock on center field. And Thomson, the left fielder recently acquired from the New York Giants, was a living legend. His unforgettable homer in the play-offs against the Dodgers had clinched the 1951 pennant for the Giants.

Even if there were an opening, Aaron would have had to battle Jim Pendleton for it. This former infielder had been bought from the Brooklyn organization as a spare outfielder, and he ranked ahead of the Mobile youth, who had turned twenty a week before spring training began.

If Aaron worried about the situation, he didn't show it. He slept as long as ever, looked somnambulant at the plate and in the field, and continued to hit like mad.

His first time at bat, in a spring exhibition game, he got a double off Carl Erskine of the Dodgers, one of the better pitchers in the National League.

Later, in spring training, he belted a home run off Curt Simmons of the Phillies, then even better than Erskine.

"What did you think of him?" Henry was asked.

Budding Star

"Who?" he said.

"Simmons."

"Was that Simmons?" Henry said.

The writers didn't know whether he was kidding them or not. Those who took him at face value wrote that he really didn't know it was Simmons when he first faced the Phillies' ace. Those who didn't made it evident they thought he was putting them on.

"He must have known it was Simmons," one said later. "He couldn't possibly not have known."

Yet after Aaron hit a home run off Robin Roberts, one of the best pitchers in baseball, he reacted in exactly the same way as after he had hit one off Simmons, Roberts' Phillies teammate.

"What did you think of Roberts?" somebody asked Aaron.

"Was that Roberts?" he said innocently.

Relaxed at the plate, relaxed in the field, almost mute in the locker room and off the field, Aaron was something of a mystery to everybody.

Some thought he couldn't make it as an outfielder. He never seemed to get a jump on the ball and never seemed to run hard enough to get it. Yet he was always under it when it came down, and he always got it back to the infield fast enough to keep hitters and base runners from taking liberties with his arm.

"What do you think of the kid?" Grimm was asked a few days after the exhibition games began in March.

"He does everything right," the Braves' manager said.

"Do you still think he'll have to go back to Toledo?" the observer asked.

Grimm simply shrugged and said, "We know what these others can do. They're established major leaguers. This boy hasn't played one big-league game yet and he's only twenty."

"Is he a future star?"

"Henry Aaron," Grimm said, "is a future superstar. He can do everything."

Not only Grimm, but John Quinn, the general manager, and John Mullen, the farm director, were fully aware of what was rapidly becoming a serious dilemma. Aaron, obviously ready, had to go back to Toledo. There was no way he could break into the Braves lineup that spring—as long as the regulars stayed healthy.

But they didn't.

On March 13, Bobby Thomson, the old Giants' hero, broke his leg in three places sliding into second base in an exhibition game against the Yankees at St. Petersburg. The Braves, who had paid a small fortune for him, were not happy. But now, out of a clear sky, there was suddenly room for Henry Aaron.

He wasn't given the job on a silver platter. The night that Thomson broke his leg, Grimm announced that Pafko would be shifted from right field to left and that Aaron and Pendleton would battle it out for the right-field job.

It was no contest. The next day Aaron got two hits against the Phillies. And the day after that, in a game against the Yankees, he hit a triple over Irv Noren's head in dead center field at Bradenton. The next time he came up, Noren played him 415 feet out, deeper than most major-league center-field barriers, including

Budding Star

Milwaukee's. That time Aaron lined a single to center which dropped so far in front of Noren that Aaron nearly made two bases on it.

As the opening of the season approached, Pafko made it evident that he preferred right field, his normal position, to left. Grimm began shifting him back and forth and had him in right when the team started North.

In the meantime, he gave Pendleton, as well as Aaron, a shot at left, but Pendleton couldn't compete with the youngster, and the Braves finally handed the job to Henry. On opening day he was in left field, batting fifth, between Pafko and Adcock.

Throughout the time the club was in Florida, Aaron had hardly opened his mouth. In Milwaukee, one of the local writers who had been with the club wrote, "Henry Aaron didn't utter a total of 100 words all spring."

After he had played a few days in the outfield, Aaron was asked by another writer how he liked it.

"I like it fine," he said. "There's less to do—especially thinking."

It was exactly the sort of remark that puzzled everyone who talked to Aaron. He made it without changing expression, yet it seemed certain that it was just another example of his quiet humor.

Another was his reply to a writer who pointed out to him one day that he was batting .275.

"Is that all?" Aaron asked.

"Well, it's pretty good for a rookie," the writer said.

"Shucks," Aaron said, "I thought I'd lead this league."

When the team arrived in Milwaukee from Florida, Aaron was so complete a stranger to the clubhouse boys that they spelled his name wrong. He walked into the Braves' room for the first time, looked around for his locker, and found that his name over it had only one *A*.

His uniform number was 5, which was normally desirable on any big-league club because it meant that the wearer was a regular. Aaron didn't like it. He wore the number all that year, then switched to 44, which he kept throughout his career.

Neither he nor the Braves got off to a particularly good start in 1954. On opening day, at Cincinnati, they lost a slugfest to the Reds, 9–8. Eddie Mathews got two homers, and practically everyone else hit well, but not Aaron. In five trips to the plate he struck out twice, grounded out, hit into a double play, and fouled out.

Later Charlie Grimm was asked what he thought of his rookie outfielder.

"I think he's great," Grimm said. "He's my left fielder."

"But he looked terrible at the plate," a writer remarked.

"He was scared to death," Grimm said. "This was his first major-league game. He'll be all right."

The Braves looked only so-so the first week of the season, losing one here, winning another there, sticking around the middle of the standings. By April 23 they were third, with four wins and three losses, a reasonable place for a pennant contender to be that early in the season.

Budding Star

The ball club went to St. Louis for a series with the Cardinals, facing Vic Raschi in the first game. Old-time New York Yankee fans remembered him for his great pitching in the years following World War II. Henry Aaron remembers him for another reason. On that afternoon of April 23, 1954, Henry hit one of Raschi's fast balls into the left-field seats for the first home run of his major-league career.

The homer was an important factor in a wild ball game that went to fourteen innings. The score was 4–4 at the end of the ninth. Aaron hit a single to drive in the Braves' fifth run in the thirteenth, but the Cardinals tied it up in their half. The Braves settled it, 7–5, with two in the fourteenth. Aaron had two singles and a home run in seven times up, his best day up to that time.

He bettered it two days later, when he paced the Braves to a 12–3 win in the last game of the series. That day he had a home run and four singles in six trips to the plate. The kid was off and running.

But he wasn't a star yet, although he had his moments and continued to show promise of future magnificence. His hitting was spotty, largely because he had trouble with curve balls. He hadn't seen too many in the minor leagues. In the majors, he saw them all the time, especially when word got around that they bothered him.

The Braves' two top pitchers, Warren Spahn, probably the best curve-ball artist in the business, and Lew Burdette, worked with him for hours. Since Spahn was a southpaw and Burdette a right-hander, they gave Aaron plenty of chance to see all kinds of curve-ball pitching. Between their patience and Henry's hard work, he gradually overcame his problem, although it took him a year and a half to do it.

During his rookie season he pulled occasional boners, one of which was worthy of the old Daffiness Boys, the inept Brooklyn Dodgers of the twenties, who once had three men on third. Aaron helped the Braves put two men there one day when he doubled into a double play.

Running with his head down, another fault he had to overcome before he could be a finished ballplayer, he decided to try for three bases without noticing that the man ahead of him wasn't sure whether to try to score or not. He decided against it, and when the third baseman got the ball, he found Braves sliding in from both directions. He tagged them both in one sweeping motion.

"Henry," Grimm said when he got back to the dugout, "you've got to watch the ball and watch who's on the bases and where. And you've got to decide when to run and when not to."

"Skipper," Aaron replied, "I can't do all that at once."

Another time, when the next batter hit a line drive that was obviously going to drop safely in deep right field, Aaron, who had been on first, lost his cap between second base and third. He could have scored easily, but he went back to pick it up—he was lucky to end up on third.

Later Grimm said, "When you have your choice between a cap and a run, you take the run."

One tough problem for Aaron was to decide when

to tag up and when to hover between bases on long fly balls. He knew that from first base he was supposed to be between first and second on a routine fly, so that he could get back to first if it were caught and move on to second if it weren't. And for a long time he thought he was supposed to do the same thing when on second.

But from there, he should have tagged up on a fly to deep right or right center, in order to go to third after the catch. Instead, he hovered, then had to scamper back to second. It took time for him to learn to plant himself on second until the ball was caught, then to try for third if he had a chance to make it.

Once he learned, he never forgot. And his good days outnumbered his bad. Some of those good days were tremendous, such as the afternoon in May when the Braves were losing a game at Chicago, 2–1, going into the ninth. Bob Rush, the Cubs' pitcher, opened the inning by walking Mathews. Aaron, batting in the cleanup spot, took two pitches, then belted the third out of the park for a 3–2 Braves victory. It was the sort of thing Henry did more and more of as the years went on.

Perhaps his greatest day of 1954 was one which ended in tragedy for him. By early September the Braves were in third place, five games behind the league-leading Giants and one in back of the second-place Dodgers. On the fifth, they went into Cincinnati for a doubleheader with the Reds. Bobby Thomson, back in action after being out most of the season, was in and out of the lineup, relieving regular outfielders when Grimm wanted to rest them. In the first game of the twin bill, Thomson started in Aaron's place in left field.

It was a weird game because the Braves took a long early lead, then blew it when the Reds got five runs in the sixth for a 6–5 lead.

Adcock tied it up with a home run in the seventh; then Thomson, hitless all day, walked. Grimm put Aaron in to run for him, and Henry scored on Crandall's double. Later, in his only time at bat, Aaron himself doubled as the Braves won an 11–8 victory.

Aaron was back in left field, batting cleanup, when the second game began. He singled in the first inning, doubled in the fourth, and drove in a run with his second single in the seventh, when the Braves scored seven runs to take an 8–7 lead.

Dave Koslo, the last of a succession of Cincinnati pitchers, was on the mound when Aaron came to bat in the ninth, his fifth time up because he had drawn a walk, but only his fourth official trip to the plate. The Braves were leading, 9–7, when Aaron pickled a Koslo pitch into deep left center, squarely in the alley between two outfielders.

He rounded first, saw he could make three bases, and barreled around second. Gus Bell, the Reds' center fielder, finally retrieved the ball and threw it to Chuck Harmon, the third baseman. The throw was a trifle late, but Henry hit the dirt, sliding in with a triple.

But he slid too hard. His spikes caught in the bag, a stab of pain shot up his leg, and every one in the ball park knew he was badly hurt. His ankle was broken, and as he was carried off in a stretcher, his

Budding Star

teammates shook their heads and muttered, "There goes the pennant."

They were right. Henry was through for the year, and so were the Braves, even though they swept the doubleheader. The injury came on the heels of a perfect batting day for Aaron—five hits in five times at bat—but the Braves never recovered from his loss. They finished third.

Henry batted .280 and hit 13 home runs, a fine performance for a twenty-year-old rookie, but not good enough to win him any national honors. Wally Moon of the Cardinals was the National League's rookie of the year, with Henry not a very close second.

But even if nobody else appreciated him, the Milwaukee baseball writers did. He was their unanimous choice for the Braves' Most Valuable Player.

5 Batting Champion

IN 1955 the major leagues established a rule prohibiting all but pitchers and catchers from reporting for spring training before March 1. At the time the rule was well publicized for no other reason than that it was new. And at the time most major-leaguers abided by it.

But several members of the Braves, including Henry Aaron, were so eager to get started that they showed up at Bradenton for spring training at least a week ahead of the March 1 deadline. During that week they did little but run, play pepper games, and simply fool around the ball park. The Braves' management had no objection; in fact, the front office was pleased to see Henry and the others so willing to get to work so early.

One day—still before March 1—there was a telegram waiting for each of the boys when he appeared at the park. Henry, who had never received a wire in his life, crumpled it up without opening it and started to throw it away when he was stopped by manager Charlie Grimm.

"Hey," Grimm said, "don't throw that wire away. Do you know who it's from?"

"No," Aaron said.

"Ford Frick," said Grimm.

"Who's he?" Henry said.

Ford Frick was the baseball commissioner. Although it was hard to believe that any ballplayer would fail to recognize his name, Aaron looked so innocently at Grimm that the Braves' manager wasn't sure whether Henry was kidding him or not.

Finally, Grimm gave him the benefit of the doubt. He shrugged his shoulders and said, "Frick's the boss . . . the big shot . . . the commissioner. Now open the envelope and read the message. It's important."

The wire informed Henry that he was thereby being fined $500 for appearing at spring training before he was supposed to. Aaron could hardly believe his eyes.

"He's fining me five hundred dollars for *working*," he said.

Each of the Braves who had shown-up with Henry was also fined $500. Everyone from the front office down was upset, but the fines stuck. There were reports later that the Braves paid the fines for their ballplayers, but these were never confirmed. In any event, it was the only time players were ever punished for violating the March 1 rule. It's still on the books, but nobody pays any attention to it, including the commissioner's office.

The Brooklyn Dodgers made a shambles of the 1955 season before it was fairly started. They won their first 10 games in a row and 22 of their first 24, practically clinching the pennant by Mother's Day. For everyone else, even the Braves, who finished second, it was a bad year.

But it wasn't a bad year for Henry Aaron, although some observers expected it to be. Baseball is famous for its sophomore jinx. Over the years, dozens of rookies looking great in their first season have had trouble in their second.

Just before the season began, Aaron was asked if he thought the sophomore jinx would hurt him.

"What's the sophomore jinx?" he said. "I never heard of it."

And he hit as if he had never heard of it. For Henry Aaron, a potential big-league star in his first season, blossomed into a full-blown star in his second. The youth from Mobile, still only twenty-one, couldn't do anything wrong. Deadly at the plate, he could hit any pitch anywhere, and he often did.

Pitchers were frightened of him, because they just didn't know how to handle him. When the Dodgers, leading the league by a mile, picked up a hurler from another club in midseason, every pitcher on the Brooklyn staff went to him and said, "How did you guys pitch Aaron?"

The new arrival shrugged his shoulders and said, "We've tried everything—and nothing works."

Bob Friend, then the Pittsburgh Pirates' ace, spent many a sleepless night worrying about Aaron.

"There's no way to pitch him." Friend said. "Get him on a curve ball once and he'll kill it the next time up. Blow a fast ball by him and you don't know what he'll do with it the next time. And he gets more hits off bad balls than most guys do off good. I've seen him hit pitches off his ear into the right-field stands."

Aaron never bunted—not that he wouldn't, but Grimm didn't want him wasting a time at bat bunting. The word soon got around, and after a while nobody expected him to bunt.

Once in Brooklyn, he twice bluffed bunts. Both times Jackie Robinson, playing third base, didn't make a move toward the plate, staying back in his regular position.

When Aaron asked him why, Robinson said, "Listen, Henry. We'd rather have you bunting in this park than swinging away and hitting one out. Any time you want to bunt, we'll give you first base just so you don't get any more."

Aaron's gentle sense of humor was never keener than the day a rookie, watching him in batting practice, noticed that he was holding his bat with the label facing the pitcher.

"Hey, Henry," the kid said, "you'd better turn the label up."

"Boy," Aaron said, "I didn't come up here to read."

One day in midseason, when Aaron was hitting around .340, somebody asked him if he felt the pitcher or the hitter had the advantage. Everybody in baseball would have said the pitcher, but not Henry.

"I figure I've got the advantage," he said. "I have a bat. All the pitcher has is a ball."

Popular with teammates and fans, Aaron was an enigma to newspapermen. Time after time they would come away from interviews shaking their heads in wonder, then write that Aaron was a hard man to understand because he never said anything.

"They think *I'm* hard to understand?" Aaron said one day. "I can't figure *them* out. They rush in, ask a couple of questions about batting, or maybe how many shrimps I can eat at one sitting, then rush out. The next day I read that I'm 'mysterious,' or 'inscrutable,' or 'not colorful.' One guy wrote that I was 'full of grave silence.' I don't think I'm that way at all, as anyone would find out if he spent a little time with me and tried to get to know me. But nobody does."

That was the year Aaron played in his first All-Star Game. The classic, one of the best ever played, was held in Milwaukee, where the American League had a 5–0 lead as the Nationals came to bat in the last of the seventh. Henry, who already had a single in his one time at bat, walked, then scored the first of two runs, which made it 5–2. In the eighth he singled again to drive in the tying run.

The Nationals finally won, 6–5, in the twelfth, when Stan Musial hit a homer into the right-field stands at County Stadium.

Although Aaron played right field most of the season—as he did during most of the rest of his career—he filled in at second base for 27 games when Danny O'Connell was hurt. He played well, if not sensationally, accepting 176 chances, taking part in 23 double plays, and making 6 errors for a .966 average.

He ended the season sixth in batting with a .314 average and tied with teammate Johnny Logan for the league lead in doubles with 37. He also led the Braves in batting, hits, and RBI's, while finishing second on the club to Eddie Mathews in home runs.

During the winter following the 1955 season, Henry heard himself praised to the skies by Lou Perini, the owner of the Braves, at the annual Baseball Writers Dinner in Milwaukee. When it was his turn to speak, he said, "Did Mr. Perini mean that before I sign my contract or after?"

Shortly after that, when he got his 1956 contract, he called John Quinn, the general manager, and said, "Mr. Quinn, haven't you sent me O'Connell's contract by mistake?"

O'Connell had batted .225.

Eventually, Aaron got the contract he wanted, considerably more than the original offer, and was quite satisfied when he reported for spring training in 1956 —on March 1.

The first thing he did on his first day at Bradenton was step into the batting cage and belt the first three pitches he saw over the left-field fence. Then the youth, who had just turned twenty-two, stepped out, saying, "Old Hank is ready."

He had a tremendous spring training, murdering practically every pitcher he faced. One day, after an exhibition game against the Dodgers at Vero Beach, somebody told Brooklyn manager Walter Alston that Aaron was batting .552 in exhibition games against his club.

"Well," Alston commented, "I see no reason why he won't keep on hitting .552 against us all year."

Alston wasn't too far wrong. Aaron actually hit .442 against the Dodgers that year. But first he went through some unfamiliar pangs of frustration, for he had left too many hits in Florida. After a short hitting streak at the beginning of the season, he went into a monumental slump, one of the worst of his entire career.

Practically all of it came during a long home stand in Milwaukee. From the heights of well over .400 Aaron dropped all the way to .167. In one stretch of sixteen games he had only 12 hits in 64 times up for a .188 average, and he batted in only six runs.

As Henry went, so went the Braves. One of the favorites to win the National League pennant, they had a short spell of prosperity at the start—just as Aaron did—then went into a steep decline. The situation got so bad that Charlie Grimm resigned as manager on June 16, to be succeeded by Fred Haney.

In the meantime, everyone worried about Aaron except Henry himself. Milwaukee fans and close observers of the club alike were concerned over his failure to hit, but Aaron just kept plugging along.

One day a visiting writer said, "Henry, your batting average is pretty low. What are you doing about it?"

"Just what I always did—keep swinging," Aaron said. "A lot of people are worried about my average, but I'm not. Anyone with a pencil can figure it out."

The writer walked off talking to himself. The cryptic answer was typical of the young man who had given it.

A hitter as great as Aaron and a club as strong as the Braves couldn't stay in the dumps forever. With Haney in charge things began to look up, and as the All-Star Game approached the Braves started moving.

Although he still wasn't hitting at his normal pace,

Batting Champion

Aaron was again picked to play for the National Leaguers. Unlike 1955, when he was one of the stars, he failed to distinguish himself, playing only a couple of innings and appearing only once at the plate.

But after the All-Star break, both Aaron and the Braves went into orbit. With everyone hitting like mad, the club won 9 straight games and 15 out of 20 during a long home stand that lasted until July 22. A week before the stand ended, Henry began a fantastic hitting streak.

It began modestly, when Henry had one single in three times at bat in the second game of a doubleheader against Pittsburgh on July 15. The next day he had two hits, one a homer off Ron Kline that beat the Pirates, 2–1. On the seventeenth, in a losing game to the Giants, Aaron went two for five, including a three-run homer. On the eighteenth, he led a 7–3 assault on Giants' pitching with a single, a double, and a triple. And on the nineteenth he contributed a single and a double as the Giants bowed again.

Now came a four-game series against the Phillies to finish the home stand. Henry had two singles and a homer in the first game, a single and a double in the second, a double and a game-winning homer in the third, and a single in the finale.

So as the Braves left home, Aaron was riding on the wings of a nine-game hitting streak. During the home stand he had collected 27 hits in 59 times up and raised his average to .336. But Henry had only begun to hit.

The road trip began in New York, where Aaron opened with two hits, the second a ninth-inning triple that beat the Giants. The next day he had a single and the day after, two singles and a home run. Then the Braves went to Philadelphia, where Henry hit a single in the first of two games and a triple in the second. That lifted his streak to 14.

One day Barbara wrote, "Don't come home unless you're over .300." As she well knew, there was no chance of his dropping below .300 even if he fell on his face in Brooklyn, the next stop on the road trip.

He didn't. In the first of four games against the Dodgers, he knocked them dead with a single, a double, a home run, and four RBI's. He had a double in the second, which was played at Ruppert Stadium in Jersey City. Two singles in the third and another in the fourth kept his streak alive as the Braves moved on to Pittsburgh.

Aaron had hit safely in 18 straight games. He made it 19 with a single in the first game, twenty with a double in the second, 21 with a single and a triple in the third, and 22 with a double and a triple in the fourth. Then the Braves went home to Milwaukee.

By this time the whole baseball world was watching his daily hit production. Although Joe DiMaggio's all-time record of 56 straight was still a long way off, Tommy Holmes' National League record of 37 was in sight.

The Braves opened against the Cubs and lost, but Aaron got a single and a double for his 23d straight. He made it 24 with two singles the next day and 25 in the first game of a doubleheader against the Cardinals on August 8. Now he was only 12 games short of Holmes' mark, set in 1945 while Holmes was playing for the Braves in Boston.

"How do you stop Henry Aaron?"

The cry had been sounded around the league for nearly three years. Early in this 1956 season it appeared as if the National League's pitching union had found the answer, but now the situation was worse than ever. Aaron was clicking out hits like clockwork, and nobody seemed able to do anything about it.

As always, Aaron didn't show the least signs of pressure. When he talked—which was as little as ever—he spoke in calm, low tones, answering questions briefly but courteously, talking and acting as if long hitting streaks were just part of a year's work. To him, they were.

"You swing the bat," he said. "You hit the ball or you don't hit the ball."

"What about the streak?" he was asked.

"It'll end," Aaron said. "They always do."

The man who stopped it at 25 games was Herman Wehmeier, a veteran St. Louis right-hander who pitched the second game of that August 8 doubleheader in Milwaukee. Aaron faced him four times without a hit, and when the game was over, all he did was shrug.

"Are you unhappy?" someone said in the locker room later. The answer made more sense than the question.

"I'm never happy when I don't hit," Henry said.

"I mean about the streak."

"No," Aaron said. "A streak is just luck. And you can't control luck."

In the 25 games, Aaron went to bat 108 times, had

44 hits, including 9 doubles, 4 triples, and 7 home runs, drove in 25 runs and batted .407. Of the 15 games the Braves won during his streak, he settled 8 with key hits, 3 of them homers in late innings.

The season progressed, and so did the Braves. By mid-August they were in the midst of a three-way pennant fight with the Dodgers and the Reds, with first one, then another, then a third moving into the lead. Everyone around Milwaukee was talking pennant, while the ballplayers around the league, especially the pitchers, were talking Aaron. He and Wally Moon of the Cardinals were fighting for the batting championship, but Aaron was much the better hitter. He worried the opposition far more than Moon did.

Someone asked Rogers Hornsby, immortal right-handed slugger of another era with whom Aaron was often compared, if he thought the youth had a weakness.

"Sure, he has a weakness," Hornsby said. "It's a pitch with something on it right across the letters and in close. But that's the batting weakness of every great hitter, regardless of what else he can or can't hit."

If anyone tried to throw pitches in close across the letters with something on it, Aaron didn't seem aware of it. When he was in a streak, he could hit anything.

One day he told a writer, "I never worry about a pitcher unless he has a knuckler," and the story appeared in print the next day. Not long after that, in the opening game of a series between the Braves and the Pirates, manager Bobby Bragan of the Pirates told Vernon Law, his starting pitcher, to throw nothing but knucklers at Aaron. Henry hit the first one out of the park.

"What do you want me to do now?" Law asked when the inning was over.

"I can't imagine," Bragan said.

Don Newcombe, the great Dodger right-hander, asked how he pitched Aaron, replied, "I try to throw the ball *under* the plate."

Through all the furor, Aaron moved serenely, not seeming to care whether he hit well or not, but actually caring very much. Asked one day what he considered his most important function for the Braves, he said, "Hitting pitchers' mistakes."

Another time somebody asked him, "What's on your mind when you go up to the plate?"

"Nothing," Aaron said.

"You must be thinking of something," the other persisted.

"When I go up to the plate," Aaron said, "I try to keep my mind absolutely clear. All I want to think about is the baseball."

His sense of humor was as sharp as ever. One day, while he was at bat in a game against the Reds, Smokey Burgess, the Cincinnati catcher, got into a terrible argument with the plate umpire over a called ball. Aaron, after listening for a few minutes, finally said, "Kindly do not agitate the arbiter. He can't be as pluperfect as you are."

That ended the argument. Both Burgess and the umpire broke up.

Aaron went into a slight slump after his batting streak, then bounced back. Over the Labor Day weekend, he killed two birds with one stone, hitting the ball so hard and so often that he helped the Braves move into a three-and-a-half-game lead while passing Moon in his personal struggle with the Cardinals' outfielder for the batting championship.

In the first game of a Labor Day doubleheader in Milwaukee, Henry had a field day against Johnny Klippstein of the Reds. With the Braves trailing, 2–0, in the fourth inning, he belted a homer to make it 2–1. In the seventh he hit another homer to make it 2–2. And in the ninth he doubled, scoring the winning run on Joe Adcock's hit.

He had a double and a home run in the second game, but the Reds had taken a 7–1 lead, and the Braves couldn't catch up. They finally lost, 7–5. Aaron's two doubles and three homers in eight times up put him ahead of Moon. And the Braves' three wins in four games put them in front of the pack.

They remained there most of the month of September. While the Reds dropped out of the race, the Dodgers slowly moved up until, on the next to last day of the season, they were only half a game behind the league-leading Braves.

That afternoon they won a doubleheader against the Pirates, putting them half a game in front of the Braves, who had a night game in St. Louis. If they could win it, the Braves would be in an exact tie with Brooklyn, with only one game to go.

Warren Spahn, their perennial 20-game winner, was on the mound against Wehmeier, the man who had stopped Aaron's hitting streak. Bruton opened the game with a single; then, with two out, Henry came to bat. With the count two and two, Wehmeier threw a slow curve that dipped as it approached the plate. Aaron, timing it perfectly, golfed it to left center for a double, and Bruton scored with the first run of the game.

For five innings, the Cardinals ate out of Spahn's hand, as the great Braves left-hander pitched hitless ball. He then retired the first two men he faced in the sixth, but the next two doubled, killing both his no-hitter and his lead.

The score was 1–1, and it stayed that way through the seventh, the eighth, the ninth, the tenth, and the eleventh as the tension built up. After Wehmeier got the Braves out in the first half of the twelfth, the Cards came up for the second half.

Spahn retired the lead-off man; then Musial doubled. The Braves' hurler walked Ken Boyer purposely to set up a double play, and it looked as if the Braves would pull one off when Rip Repulski hit a sharp grounder to Eddie Mathews at third base.

Just as Mathews got set for it, the ball hit a pebble, caromed off Mathews' knee and slithered out to left field for a double. Musial scored the winning run, and the Braves were a full game behind Brooklyn.

Even though they were mathematically still in the race, the Braves knew they were beaten. All that could save them was a combination of a victory over the Cardinals and a Dodgers' loss to the Pirates, which would put them into a tie with Brooklyn for first place.

The Braves did what they could—beat the Cardinals —but the Dodgers didn't cooperate. They slapped down the Pirates again, and it was all over.

The loss of the pennant was such a bitter disappointment to Henry that the winning of the batting title was small solace. He ended up at .328 to become the second youngest champion in National League history. Only Pete Reiser of the 1941 Dodgers, who also won at twenty-two, was younger, and that by a month and fourteen days.

Henry, the only man in the league with 200 hits, also led in that department, as well as in doubles. It had been a great season for him, and he was sure of another substantial raise for 1957.

He would rather have won the pennant.

6 Most Valuable Player

IN 1955 Aaron was fined for showing up at spring training too early. In 1957 he was challenged by his manager for showing up too late.

"What happened?" Haney asked.

"I was late catching the train from Mobile," Henry said.

"Why didn't you start out earlier?" the manager demanded.

"Because then I would have been here too soon," Aaron calmly replied.

Haney didn't know whether to laugh or get mad. Since it was virtually impossible ever to get mad at Aaron, he finally laughed and forgot about it.

Aaron was beginning to approach big money brackets. For the 1957 season he had signed a contract reported to be $28,500, which, in view of the fact that he had added a batting championship to all his other accomplishments, was nowhere nearly what he was worth. In later years he got up close or into six figures for an annual salary, but the process took longer that it should have.

Again, as in 1956, he had a great spring training season. Wherever he went, he belted the ball hard and often, not even being slowed too much by a sprained ankle. The injury kept him out of seven exhibition games, yet he ended the training season with a .390 batting average and 11 home runs.

Obviously, he belonged in a power spot in the batting order, but Haney decided to bat him second. One reason was that the Braves had power all up and down the line; another was that Haney felt Aaron would pile up more times at bat.

Henry accepted the move with reservations, because he felt he could do himself and the team more good in the number three or four slot. However, he accepted the situation gracefully, even justifying it in a way.

"I'm no home-run hitter really," he said. "The ones I get are accidents. I'll never drive in one hundred runs batting second, but we have a few other guys who can do that."

Yet when asked if he had any personal goals for 1957, he replied, "Three. I'd like to hit .350, get thirty homers, and drive in one hundred runs."

The season wasn't two weeks old before Haney, realizing his mistake, shifted Aaron into the cleanup spot where he belonged. There he all but ripped the league apart, changing his home-run sights as he went along.

When he had 19 in 59 games, he said, "Could be I'll hit thirty-five by just swinging the way I have been all year." And by July, as he approached 30, he predicted the possibility of hitting 40. He wound up with 44.

The Braves started the season with a team which, if it had remained healthy, was capable of running away with the pennant race. Big Joe Adcock was on first base, Danny O'Connell on second, Johnny Logan at short, Eddie Mathews at third, Bobby Thomson and Andy Pafko in left field, Bill Bruton in center, and Henry Aaron in right.

Adcock, Mathews, and Aaron were power hitters who could often break up a game with one swing of the bat. All the others except O'Connell were home-run threats at one time or another. Bruton was one of the speed demons of the league, and everyone else but Adcock was dangerous on the bases.

The first-string catcher, Del Crandall, who could hit, throw, and think, ranked after only Roy Campanella of the Dodgers as the best all-around receiver in the league. Behind Spahn and Burdette, the toughest one-two pitching punch in baseball, the Braves had more fine pitchers that they could use, including Bob Buhl, Gene Conley, Ray Crone, Dave Jolly, Don McMahon, Red Murff, Taylor Phillips, Juan Pizarro, Bob Trowbridge, and Ernie Johnson.

The Braves had everything—pitching, power, defense, speed—and most of the nation's baseball experts picked them to win. They started out at a pace comparable to that of the Dodgers two years before but lacked the Dodgers' luck. For even though the Braves won their first 5 games and 9 of their first 10, the best they could do with the season two weeks old was second place. The Reds won 12 of their first 13 games.

Aaron started the season with a 34-ounce bat, 2 ounces lighter than usual, and the only people who regretted the change were opposing pitchers. Up to then, Henry had always started with a 36-ounce bat and worked down to 34, but he decided the lighter bat would save him the pain of early-season slumps; this was just what happened.

He performed some mighty feats with that light bat, hitting safely and scoring in every one of the first seven games of the season, while belting three home runs and batting .391. And as the first weeks of the season progressed, he didn't tail off very much.

He was a factor in many Milwaukee victories, as any baseball observer could see simply by looking at the box scores. He beat the Reds with his first home run of the season—the only Cincinnati loss in more than two weeks. The next day his bases-loaded single in the tenth inning beat the Giants.

In another game his ninth-inning three-run homer tied the Pirates; then he tripled in the eleventh and scored the winning run on a sacrifice fly. The night after that, he beat the Pirates with five straight hits. Two nights later he crushed the Dodgers with two singles, a double, and a homer. Then he hit two home runs and a double to beat the Pirates.

And so it went, not game after game, but two, sometimes three games a week. When Aaron took over the cleanup spot, following Mathews, the two sluggers formed what eventually became the most lethal one-two batting combination baseball has ever known. Before they were separated, when Mathews was traded years later, they had passed even the immortal New York

Yankee home-run twins, Babe Ruth and Lou Gehrig.

As always, Aaron was the talk—and the scourge—of the league. One day manager Birdie Tebbetts of the Reds said, "Logan and Crandall murder my ball club."

"How about Aaron?" he was asked.

"Aaron," Tebbets said, "murders everybody."

By this time Aaron had long since started wearing number 44, which he carried on his uniform back for the rest of his career. After he had walloped the Dodgers practically single-handedly, one of his victims said, "That number he wears really means four for four."

Despite years of bitter experience with Aaron, managers and pitchers still sometimes thought they had his number. When the Giants held him to two singles in three games, manager Bill Rigney told one of the New York writers, "I think we've finally learned how to pitch to Henry Aaron."

In the next six games in which he faced the Giants, Aaron had 12 hits, including 2 homers, in 27 times up for an average of .444.

One observer asked manager Bobby Bragan of the Pirates if there was any way he would change Aaron's batting stance.

"You don't change a hitter like Aaron," Bragan replied. "He knows more about hitting than you do. He's the greatest right-handed batter I've ever seen, up to and including Willie Mays."

Some pitchers tried to intimidate Aaron, but that usually backfired. One night, when Henry came up after doubling off Johnny Antonelli of the Giants, Antonelli yelled, "Hey, Henry, you can afford to lose some teeth."

"Yeah," Aaron yelled back, "but can you?"

Antonelli threw a fast ball at his whiskers, and Aaron hit it 450 feet into the upper deck of New York's Polo Grounds. He had three homers and seven RBI's as the Braves belted the Giants, 13–3, in that game.

The Reds stayed on top of the National League pack for twenty-three days, slipped back for a day, got back up for two more, and from then until the All-Star Game the lead changed hands ten times.

In the meantime, a series of events, both good and bad, radically altered the powerful lineup which had made the Braves look like sure pennant winners before the season had even begun. The first was a trade with the Giants in mid-June which looked risky at the time but turned out to be a key move.

Although the front office had pinned high hopes on Danny O'Connell, Haney was not satisfied with him at second base. The Giants had just acquired Red Schoendienst from the Cardinals during the previous winter, and Schoendienst was very unhappy. He loved St. Louis and had hoped to spend his entire career there. He was second only to Musial in popularity, and his trade had been a shock both to him and Cardinal fans.

The Braves knew he had been an outstanding switch-hitter and a fine second baseman at St. Louis, but there was a question of whether or not he still was. A skinny, frail-looking thirty-four, he hadn't been doing well in New York, and there was talk he might be through. But the Braves, although they had to give up a lot to get him, decided it was worth the chance.

They sent Bobby Thomson back to the Polo Grounds, the scene of his greatest triumphs, along with O'Connell and Ray Crone, a starting pitcher, virtually giving up three regulars for one. Yet they could spare all three. Thomson was only a part-time outfield regular. O'Connell, of course, would be replaced at second by Schoendienst. And the Braves pitching was so strong that Crone would hardly be missed.

It turned out to be a magnificent deal for Milwaukee. Schoendienst not only had one of his best seasons at the plate and in the field, but was an inspirational leader who bolstered up the whole ball club. He was exactly the man the Braves needed, especially in the light of subsequent events.

For less than two weeks after Schoendienst joined the ball club, Joe Adcock broke his right leg sliding into second base in a game against the Phillies. This blow, which cut the Braves' power alley down to two men—Aaron and Mathews—also robbed the club of an experienced first baseman at a time when he was needed most.

With Adcock gone for the better part of the season the Braves were forced to put Frank Torre, a good hitter but a rookie, on first base. It was then that Schoendienst proved that his value went beyond his mechanical ability to play ball. The veteran second baseman helped Torre in a dozen ways and steadied him down at a time when the kid might have shown signs of serious jitters.

Almost as if to pick up the slack caused by the loss

of Adcock, Aaron hit the ball harder than ever. By the All-Star Game he was batting .352 and leading the league in almost everything.

"How far do you think he'll go?" a writer asked Haney one day.

"Who knows?" the manager replied. "Maybe he'll hit .360, maybe .400. He's capable of anything."

After the All-Star Game, in which Aaron was now a fixture, the Braves suddenly suffered a whole series of major and minor disasters. First, Bill Bruton, their marvelously smooth center fielder, tore cartilages in his knee, finishing him for the year. This meant a complete reshuffling of the outfield.

Henry moved from right field to center, where he remained for the balance of the season. The Braves then brought two rookies up from their Wichita farm club, Wes Covington and Bob Hazle, installing Covington in right and keeping Hazle in reserve to spell Andy Pafko in left. This was fortunate, since Pafko was hurt a few days later and Hazle caught fire when he took Pafko's place. Over a 41-game period the kid hit a fantastic .403 before the rest of the league caught up with him.

Then Johnny Logan was hurt, and Haney had to replace him with Felix Mantilla, who could hit but was a shaky infielder. At that point the Braves' lineup had Torre, Schoendienst, Mantilla, and Mathews in the infield and Covington, Aaron and Hazle in the outfield, but Haney still had to do a lot of improvising. Several times he moved Del Crandall out from behind the bat to play first base or one of the outfield spots, replacing him as the catcher with either Carl Sawatski or Del Rice.

Instead of falling apart, the Braves seemed to thrive on adversity. With the help of a 10-game winning streak, they remained in the thick of a wild battle which, on July 29, found only 2½ games separating the top five teams—the Braves, the Dodgers, the Cardinals, the Reds, and the Phillies.

One day in early August, with the Braves trailing by three runs at Philadelphia, Aaron came up in the seventh inning and rocketed a long outfield drive to chase Schoendienst home from second base. As Henry was running from first to second, he saw he could make three bases, but he had to slide to do it. His foot hooked hard into the bag, and the Braves' players in the nearby dugout gasped as they heard him groan, then watched in horror as he tried unsuccessfully to get up under his own power.

"Oh, no," said Haney. "Not him."

Helped off the field, Aaron lay on the rubbing table in the locker room while the trainer bent over him.

"Is it broken?" asked Haney.

"I don't know," was the reply. "It'll have to be X-rayed."

There was no break, but ankle tendons were sprained. According to the doctor, it would be two weeks before Henry could get back into action.

Much as he regretted the loss of even a single day, Aaron welcomed the layoff because it gave him time to help Barbara move into their new house just outside Milwaukee. The decision to move permanently out of Mobile was a natural one, since there were no opportunities there for Negroes, even a Henry Aaron.

The Aarons now had four children, including Larry, infant survivor of premature twins, the other of whom had died at birth. The size of their growing family had also been a strong factor in the Aarons' decision to move North. They couldn't find a suitable house in Mobile big enough for their needs.

At first, Henry had been nervous about looking for a home in Milwaukee. Realistic about his color, he didn't know what effect a purchase by him might have on white neighbors. As it turned out, there were no problems. The people who lived nearby welcomed him.

Not that Aaron had any illusions. Right after he moved, he told friends, "My neighbors are real nice—warm, friendly folks. I couldn't have picked a more perfect place to live. But I don't think the average colored person could live there. They accept me because I'm a baseball player."

Once the family had been installed, Aaron turned back to the business of playing ball. Refusing to accept the doctor's decision that he wouldn't be ready for two weeks, he began appearing at the ball park in less than one. Eight days after suffering his ankle injury in Philadelphia, Henry felt strong enough to go back into action.

The Brooklyn Dodgers were in town, and neither they nor Aaron would ever forget that series. Henry hit a two-run homer in the ninth off Clem Labine to win the first game. The next day, in the opener of a doubleheader, Henry knocked Don Newcombe out of the box with a three-run homer, then won the game with a two-run double off Ed Roebuck. In the second game of the twin bill, Henry's double off Don Drysdale tied the score in the eighth inning; then Henry scored the winning run on Covington's single.

By this time even Red Schoendienst, Stan Musial's closest friend and former roommate, had seen enough of Aaron to be convinced of his greatness as a hitter.

"Henry is the best right-handed batter I've ever seen," Schoendienst said. Then he added the supreme accolade: "Musial is the best left-hander, but Aaron has more power."

With Aaron back, the Braves began pulling away from the pack until, as Labor Day approached, they led by six-and-a-half games. Then they went into a tailspin so steep that baseball skeptics freely predicted they would blow the pennant, and Milwaukee fans died a thousand deaths.

They sputtered and stuttered, backed and filled, and in one disastrous week lost two games for every one they won. On September 15, having dropped 8 out of their last 11, they appeared surely to be on a toboggan ride to oblivion.

Then, with Henry leading the way, they did an about-face. On the sixteenth, in Milwaukee, they played the Phillies, who had already beaten them in the first two games of a three-game series. Batting fifth, Aaron had two singles in four times up and drove in a run as the Braves won a 5–1 victory.

Henry took charge again when the Giants came to town for the first of two games. Batting in the cleanup spot, he led off the second inning with a double off Curt Barclay, then scored on a home run by Joe Adcock, who had just returned to the lineup. In the fifth Aaron singled, and in the eighth he smashed his 41st home run of the year. The Braves won that one, 3–1, and took their third in a row the next day by an 8–2 score.

They went to Chicago for a weekend series of three games with the Cubs. In the first Aaron had a double and a single and drove in a run in a 3–0 win. In the second he collected two singles and an RBI in a 6–2 win. And in the third his 42d homer helped the Braves to a 9–7 win.

When the Braves clinched the pennant with Henry's 43d home run in the eleventh inning of their September 23 game against the Cardinals at Milwaukee, it was their seventh straight victory, a streak in which Aaron was clearly the outstanding star. He hit safely in every game, had 14 for 28, including a double and 3 homers for a .500 average, and drove in 8 runs.

To top everything off, he made his 44th and final home run of the year a grand slam off Sam Jones of the Cardinals. It was a fitting finale to a magnificent season.

While the Braves were running away with the pennant, which they captured by eight games over the second-place Cardinals, Aaron was winning every major batting honor except the batting championship. After fighting Stan Musial most of the way, he suffered a late-season slump to finish in a third-place tie with Frank Robinson of the Reds at .322. Musial won at .351, and Willie Mays was second at .333.

But nobody was anywhere near Henry in home runs or runs batted in, the other two legs of the Triple

Crown. His 44 homers and 132 RBI's topped both leagues. So did his 118 runs and 369 total bases. And for the second of eight straight years, he hit at least one home run in every National League ball park.

The Braves faced the mighty New York Yankees in the World Series, which opened in New York on October 2. If they were a bit jittery, they were in good company. No National League team opening a series in Yankee Stadium for the first time was ever quite comfortable, especially in those days when the Yankees were all but invincible. Yankee power and prestige and the vast crowds in the huge stadium crushed many a great ball club before a pitch was thrown.

Furthermore, the Braves had little World Series experience. Only three of them—Red Schoendienst of the 1946 Cardinals, Warren Spahn of the 1948 Boston Braves, and Andy Pafko of the 1952 Brooklyn Dodgers—had ever played in a Series, and only Pafko had ever played a Series game in the stadium.

Spahn, sole Milwaukee survivor of the 1948 Braves, was the opening-day pitcher, facing the Yankees' Whitey Ford. When the Yankees won a 3–1 victory, the baseball world shrugged knowingly and waited for the massacre that seemed sure to follow.

But Henry Aaron triggered a Braves victory in the second game. He tripled in the second inning, scored on Adcock's single, and the Braves went on to win, 4–2, behind Lew Burdette. That took them out of the forbidding Yankee Stadium and back to the familiar Milwaukee County Stadium all even in a Series which now no longer looked like a rout by the Yankees.

Aaron's triple was his second hit of the Series (he

had singled in the first game). His two hits in eight trips at Yankee Stadium was hardly up to his normal standard, but he moved into high gear as soon as he got home, and from then on, he was the hardest and most consistent hitter in the Series.

After a day off, the third game was played on October 5. Except for Aaron, who had a home run and a single in the five times he faced Don Larsen of the Yankees, it was a disaster for the Braves. In the only game in which the Yankees really teed off on Milwaukee pitching, they coasted to a 12–3 triumph.

Once again the Yankees were one game up, but this time the experts weren't so quick to hand them the Series. The Braves' victory at Yankee Stadium had given then the confidence they needed to keep things under control. They were playing at home. Spahn was ready to pitch again. Aaron was hitting. And his slugging partner, Eddie Mathews, who hadn't had a hit in the first three games, was a sleeping giant who might explode any minute.

Facing Spahn was Tom Sturdivant, a strong-armed right-hander, and the Yankees gave him a quick 1–0 lead in the first inning. In the second Aaron beat out an infield hit, but he was forced at second. There was no more offensive action on either side until the Braves' half of the fourth.

After Logan walked, the hit-starved Mathews finally came to life, belting a double, which sent Logan to third. This brought up Aaron for the second time in the ball game. Henry took Sturdivant's first two pitches, one for a strike, the other for a ball. But when the third pitch, a fast ball, came in, he slammed it high and far to left field. While a full house of County Stadium fans went wild, the ball soared over the screen for a three-run homer. Frank Torre followed with another homer, and the Braves took a 4–1 lead.

It lasted until the first of the ninth, when Spahn suddenly wobbled. He put two men on base, then threw a home-run pitch to Elston Howard. That made the score 4–4 and sent the game into extra innings. When the Yankees scored in their half of the tenth on a walk and Hank Bauer's triple, the Braves were really in trouble.

By this time the veteran Tommy Byrne was pitching for the Yankees. When he hit pinch hitter Nippy Jones on the foot, manager Casey Stengel pulled him out and put in Bob Grim. Mantilla, who ran for Jones, went to second on Schoendienst's sacrifice and scored the tying run on Logan's double. That brought up Eddie Mathews.

First Mathews thrilled the crowd with a line shot to deep left that barely landed foul. Then he pulled another long one to right, but that was also foul. Finally, after taking two pitches for called balls, he sent the whole town home happy with a long home run to right which gave the Braves a 7–5 victory and evened the series.

The fifth game—and the last at Milwaukee—was a tight duel between Burdette and Ford which Aaron had a big hand in settling. He came up in the sixth inning of a scoreless tie with two out and Mathews on first and lined a hit to right center. Mathews went to third, then scored the only run of the game on Adcock's single. It was Burdette's second victory of the Series.

The teams went back to New York with the Braves leading, three games to two. The Yankees, behind starter Bob Turley and reliever Bobby Shantz, won a 3–2 victory in the sixth game, but it wasn't Aaron's fault. Enos Slaughter robbed him of a double with a fine catch in the first inning. He singled to left center in the fourth. And in the seventh he rocketed his second homer of the Series into the bullpen in left.

With the Series down to the seventh and final game, the Braves were in trouble because Spahn, who was scheduled to pitch, got the flu. Haney had no choice but to go with Burdette again. The big right-hander had already won two games and had had only two days' rest.

He breezed to his easiest win of the Series, a 5–0 shutout to make the Braves master of all they surveyed. When they arrived home, they were greeted at Milwaukee's airport by 20,000 screaming fans, who celebrated all that night. The baseball-mad city never really stopped celebrating all that year.

Because Burdette had become the first pitcher in nearly forty years to win three complete games in the same World Series, Aaron's accomplishments were inclined to be overlooked. But Henry had enjoyed a remarkable Series. Besides playing flawless ball in center field, he led both teams in batting, hits, home runs, runs batted in, and total bases. He ended the Series with 11 for 28, 3 homers, 7 RBI's 22 total bases, and a .393 average, and he collected at least one hit in each of the seven games.

The crowning honor came in midwinter, when the Baseball Writers of America named him the National

League's Most Valuable Player. When he beat out Stan Musial by nine votes, Musial said, "He deserved it. I've had my share of honors and I have nothing but praise for him."

As for Henry, he came as close as he ever had to showing real signs of emotion. When he could gather his thoughts, he said, "I think this is the greatest thrill of all for me. It sort of puts a guy on the baseball honor roll permanently."

He was quite right. The MVP award does "sort of put a guy on the baseball honor roll permanently." But Henry was only twenty-three years old. The best years were still ahead.

7 Jaded Champions

THERE IS NO THRILL like the thrill of a first championship. Once it is won, nothing can ever take its place; no subsequent championships can ever compare with it. With the Milwaukee Braves, there was only one first time. Anything they did after that thrill-packed 1957 season would be anti-climatic.

During the winter that followed, Braves' players who lived in or near Milwaukee were wined, dined, toasted, flattered, and kowtowed to. Nothing was too good for heroes like Aaron, Mathews, Logan and the others who had moved to the city from their original home towns. Every word they uttered was a pearl of wisdom, every move they made a stroke of genius.

Nor, in the minds of the good people of Milwaukee, could any of their heroes ever do anything wrong. They were the champions, the kings, number one. Their slightest wish was Milwaukee's command.

The city's fans were confident that their pets would

be champions forever. Indeed, Lou Perini, the wealthy Boston contractor who owned the club, predicted at the annual Baseball Writers dinner that the Braves would win at least five more pennants in a row. They would be to the National League what the Yankees were to the American.

All winter long the Aarons' home was a mecca for kids in the neighborhood. Everyone was a baseball fan, and Henry was the hero to end all heroes. He could go anywhere, do anything, have whatever he wanted.

He really didn't want much. Except for a few weeks with Lefty Miller, an old friend from his Northern League days, who invited him on an annual hunting trip in South Dakota, he was around Milwaukee a good part of the time. He liked his home and the people around it, and he and his family were completely contented that winter.

The Braves gave him a good raise in pay after the usual jockeying back and forth that always came at contract time. But by 1958 Henry was at or near the $40,000 figure, and there would be more as the years went along. The ball club was on top of the world, and Henry was right on top with it.

The Braves breezed through spring training, but there were signs of trouble when the 1958 season began. Bill Bruton, out all the last half of the 1957 season with his knee injury, still wasn't ready by opening day, and Aaron had to start in center field. It took Bruton six weeks to get back. Wes Covington suffered thigh and knee injuries and was out half the season. So was Bob Buhl, who had arm trouble from spring training.

And Red Schoendienst, the club's inspirational leader from the moment he came to the Braves from the Giants the year before, first broke a finger, then was constantly set back by extreme fatigue. He played the last six weeks of the season on his nerve. When it was over, he was found to be suffering from tuberculosis.

Aaron got off to a horrible start—the worst of his career. Neither he nor anyone else knew what was wrong, but there seemed surely to be something. After 13 games he was batting .264, and by the end of May he was down to .230.

Almost from the beginning of the season he had a nagging toothache, but he didn't mention it because it seemed unimportant. Only when it flared up did he go to the doctor. He had a badly abscessed tooth, but even after it was removed, his slump continued.

Manager Fred Haney asked Paul Waner to go to Milwaukee from his home in Sarasota, Florida, to see if he could find anything wrong with Aaron. Waner, the Braves' spring training batting coach, had been one of the greatest hitters of baseball history when he played for the Pittsburgh Pirates of the twenties.

He watched Aaron for three days, then told Haney, "Leave him alone. He'll pull out of it."

Before going home to Florida, Waner assured Henry there was nothing wrong. He was swinging properly, doing everything just as he always had, and the hits would start dropping in. A little patience was all he needed.

Waner wasn't gone a week when Henry suddenly caught fire. Starting with the last game of a series against the Giants, when he got 2 singles, he went into a streak of 11 hits in 13 times up. From then on, he was himself, the terror of all pitchers all over the National League. It had taken nearly half a season, but, as he used to say himself, old Hank was finally ready.

When Aaron got untracked, so did the ball club. Although never far from the top, the Braves failed to get away to the start they expected. They struggled along with substitutes who had to do the work of regulars unable to play.

The pitching staff, hard hit by the loss of Buhl, was also plagued by Burdette's failure to win. The hero of the 1957 World Series was having a tougher time getting started than Henry Aaron. For the first two months of the season, he couldn't seem to do much of anything right.

Then, like Aaron, he caught fire, and he ended up with a 20-game winning season. But his success was a long time coming, just as Henry's was.

Unfamiliar and seldom seen names appeared in the Braves' lineup during those early months of the season. Mel Roach, Harry Hanebrink, Felix Mantilla, the aging Andy Pafko, and Frank Torre saw much more action than they expected to.

Warren Spahn, steady and great as ever, got help from boys like Joey Jay and Juan Pizarro and Carlton Willey. The Braves' pitching rotation was a matter of conjecture from week to week, as Haney juggled it with the skill of the old master he was.

To everyone's surprise, the hottest team in the league up to the All-Star Game was the Giants, newly shifted from New York to San Francisco. Some thought the change of scenery was responsible for the surge, but this, argued others, couldn't have been the reason. Otherwise, why would the Dodgers, who had just moved from Brooklyn to Los Angeles, be in last place? It was that kind of a puzzling, crazy-quilt season.

If the Giants had been a solid ball club, they would have won the pennant going away. But not being solid, they faltered, then folded in the second half of the season. There wasn't much they could do. They simply weren't that good a club.

Haney had kept the Braves just close enough to pounce when the proper time came. From mid-July on, they were never more than three games off the top. As the dog days of August closed in, they shot past the Giants, and after that nobody caught them.

They clinched the pennant on September 21, almost one year to the day after they had clinched the 1957 flag. As usual, Henry Aaron, now long out of his slump, was the batting star. In the fifth inning of a game at Cincinnati he belted a two-run double off Brooks Lawrence. Two innings later he hit a two-run homer, his 30th of the season, off Tom Acker to give the Braves a 6–5 victory.

The second-place Pirates lost that day to eliminate themselves from the pennant race. The Braves raced on to win over them by eight games. The fading Giants finished third.

Milwaukee celebrated the winning of the pennant, but with the somewhat jaded restraint of veteran victors. There was a modest crowd at the airport to greet the Braves, but nothing like the mob of 20,000 that had met them on their return from the World Series the year before. A proper civic ceremony was well attended, but the uninhibited joy of the 1957 victory was missing.

Milwaukee, having tasted victory once, was already too used to winning to get excited.

Considering his shaky start, Aaron ended up with a real flourish. He batted .326 to finish fourth behind Richie Ashburn of the Phillies, Willie Mays of the Giants, and Stan Musial of the Cardinals. He had 30 home runs, his second best season, and 95 RBI's, his third best.

For the second year in a row, the Braves met the Yankees in the World Series. After what had happened in 1957, they felt they had nothing to fear. They had beaten the Yankees in a Series that opened in Yankee Stadium. This time, in a Series that would open in Milwaukee, how could they lose?

How indeed? Largely by overconfidence. If any ball club was beaten by its own complacency, the Braves were in the 1958 World Series against the Yankees.

Yet individual Braves starred, and no one ballplayer—nor, for that matter, the manager—could have been blamed for what actually turned out to be one of the great upsets of Series history. The Braves won the first two games and three of the first four, yet managed to blow the Series.

It wasn't Henry Aaron's fault. He had nine hits for a .333 average and a hand in several key runs. It wasn't Bill Bruton's. His .412 mark led both teams in batting. It wasn't Red Schoendienst's. Tuberculosis and all, he had a triple and three doubles and a .300

average. It wasn't Warren Spahn's. He pitched three games and won two of them. It wasn't Lew Burdette's. He pitched three of the other four games and became the first pitcher in Series history to hit a grand-slam home run. It wasn't even Eddie Mathews'. Although he struck out eleven times, he had four hits and drove in three runs.

Perhaps it was history's. For, even though the Braves themselves might not have realized it, they were bucking a baseball tradition that went back thirty-six years. No National League team had won two straight World Series since the New York Giants of 1921 and 1922.

Or, more probably, it was the Yankees. They didn't like being underdogs. And they had experience far beyond that of the Braves. They were used to winning, used to the pressure cooker of World Series competition. The 1958 Series was their fourth seven-game series in succession. Having lost two of the previous three, they were determined not to lose this one.

One question that puzzled many observers of that 1958 Series was why the Braves' pitching staff dwindled so suddenly to two men. Spahn and Burdette pitched six of the seven games, alternating in the last four. Manager Fred Haney seemed to have lost faith in practically everyone else. Other than the two aces, only Bob Rush started a game for the Braves.

Regardless of who won, it was one of the most interesting World Series ever played. Two games went ten innings. The uphill climb of the Yankees from two games down to eventual victory won for them un-Yankee-like sympathy all over the country.

Jaded Champions 95

This was not one of the great Yankee teams. On the contrary, even manager Casey Stengel described it as "a bunch of guys who will drop fly balls and do the wrong things." Man for man, the Yankees didn't compare to the Braves.

Spahn, of course, pitched the opener for Milwaukee. Except for Pafko, who started in Bruton's place in center field, the club looked familiar to all Braves followers — Adcock, Schoendienst, Logan, and Mathews in the infield; Crandall behind the bat; and Pafko, Aaron and Covington in the outfield. Haney used Pafko in center field because of his experience. Bruton, out the last half of the previous season, had never played in a World Series.

Whitey Ford opened the series for the Yankees, who had Yogi Berra catching, Moose Skowron at first base, Gil McDougald at second, Tony Kubek at short, Andy Carey at third, and Hank Bauer, Mickey Mantle, and Elston Howard in the outfield.

There were some shifts in these lineups as the Series progressed. Bruton batted for Pafko in the eighth inning of the first game and remained in center field for the rest of the Series. Frank Torre, a left-handed batter, played first in place of Adcock when right-handers were pitching.

Stengel shifted more, as he usually did. He platooned Norm Siebern in left field with Howard, used Jerry Lumpe at second, moved McDougald to third a couple of times, and changed his batting order almost every game.

Spahn and Ford battled on even terms for most of the first game. The Yankees scored all three of their runs on homers, the first a solo by Skowron in the fourth inning, the second a two-run belt by Bauer in the fifth.

Henry Aaron fanned his first time up, then scored the tying run for the Braves in their half of the fourth. Aaron walked, went to second on a passed ball, to third on an infield out, and scored on Crandall's hit. The Braves came up with a second run in that inning to take a short-lived 2—1 lead, which they lost on Bauer's homer.

So when the Braves came up in their half of the eighth, they were trailing, 3–2. Mathews opened the inning by walking; then Aaron chased him to third with a double. After Adcock fanned, Covington sent Mathews home on a sacrifice fly to tie the game at 3–3. It stayed that way through the ninth and the Yankee half of the tenth.

The Braves won it in the tenth on singles by Adcock, Crandall, and Bruton, and for the moment, at least, the full house of Milwaukee fans went home happy.

The next day they went home happier after the Braves jumped on Bob Turley and a couple of Yankee relief pitchers for seven runs in the first inning. The big blow was Burdette's grand slam, after which the right-hander coasted to a 13–6 victory. Mantle hit two homers and Bauer his second of the Series, but the Yankees were too far behind to do any business.

Aaron had a reasonable, if not sensational, day at the plate. After walking and scoring in the first inning and grounding out twice, he beat out an infield hit in the seventh and singled to right in the eighth.

The scene shifted to Yankee Stadium, with Rush

facing Don Larsen of the Yankees, a game which Henry Aaron would just as soon forget. He had no hits in three times up, the first blank he ever drew in Series competition. The Braves lost a 4–0 decision, as Bauer hit his third homer. And Aaron, for one of the few times in his career, pulled a ludicrous boner.

It happened in the sixth inning after Schoendienst singled and Aaron walked. The next batter, Covington, had a solid base hit to right, and Henry ran to third—where he met Schoendienst, who had started for the plate, then, seeing he couldn't make it, had headed back toward third. When he saw Aaron there, he started for the plate again, while Henry turned back toward second.

Eventually, Schoendienst was run down between third and home, Aaron ended up back on second, and instead of having the bases full and one out, the Braves had men on first and second with two out.

"It was my most embarrassing experience," Henry said later. "I forgot all about Schoendienst. Then I got so confused I didn't even make it to third while they were running him down."

Spahn pitched a classic two-hitter the next day to get the Braves back into the victory column. Once again he and Ford were hooked up in a tight pitching duel in the early stages of the game. The Braves scored a run in the seventh, another in the eighth, and a third in the ninth for a 3–0 victory.

Now the Braves, who had won three out of four, began talking in terms of closing the Series out in New York the next day. Plenty of experts agreed with them. The Yankees had looked pretty bad. Although hitting well, their pitching had been below par, while that of the Braves had been superb. Burdette, well rested after three days on the bench, was ready to go again. All Stengel had to throw at the Braves was Bob Turley, who hadn't lasted an inning in the second game.

It was no contest. While Turley was throwing a shutout at the Braves, his mates collected seven runs, and the Series returned to Milwaukee with the Braves still holding a lead of three games to two.

Despite the advantage, there was an air of something akin to panic about the Braves. Everyone seemed to sense impending disaster. The Yankees had already made a good comeback. Now there was a feeling that they would make it a great one.

For the third time in the Series, Warren Spahn faced Whitey Ford, with each having but two days' rest. The game started on a sour note for the Braves when Hank Bauer led off with his fourth home run of the Series. However, all wasn't lost yet because in the Braves' half of the first inning Aaron singled to drive in Schoendienst with the tying run.

In the next eight innings each team had another run, and Aaron a rare hit—a bunt in the third inning that caught the Yankees flatfooted. At the end of the ninth the score was 2-2, and for the second time in the Series, Spahn found himself going into extra innings against relief pitcher Ryne Duren.

For Spahn it was just one inning too many. Gil McDougald led it off with a home run that gave the Yankees a 3-2 lead, and they picked up another run before the session was over. When the Braves came

Jaded Champions

up for their half of the tenth, they were trailing, 4–2.

They tried, and failed by only one run, for Aaron's third single of the game drove Logan home. Then Duren slammed the door, and it was all over. The Yanks won, 4–3, to even the Series.

There was more than just something akin to panic in the Braves' locker room the next day. Stunned by what happened in the previous two games, the Braves seemed to have lost all hope. While the Yankees confidently went through their pregame practice workout, the Braves went through the motions, literally beaten before they started.

Yet they hardly disgraced themselves. For seven innings Burdette and Turley battled it out to a 2–2 deadlock. Then, in the eighth, the roof fell in. Berra doubled, Howard singled, Carey singled, Skowron hit one over the left field fence, and that was it. The four runs that streamed across the plate made heroes of the Yankees and goats of the Braves.

It was an unhappy finish to an otherwise magnificent season.

8 So Near and Yet So Far

EVEN THOUGH Red Schoendienst, their second baseman and inspirational leader, was in a St. Louis hospital recovering from tuberculosis when the 1959 season began, the Braves were expected to win the pennant easily.

Seldom, in fact, had any team begun a pennant race such overwhelming favorites. Everyone with any interest in baseball—fans, writers, players, managers, executives—considered the Braves a sure thing. A writers' poll conducted by the *Sporting News,* the game's bible, showed the scribes more than two to one in favor of Milwaukee. Fan polls and private polls among players and managers gave the Braves a bigger edge than that. About the only people who weren't sure were the Braves themselves, to say nothing of Fred Haney, their manager. No manager likes to see his club top-heavy favorites. That means anything less than a championship will be considered failure.

So Near and Yet So Far

The Braves had already won two straight pennants. Only two National League teams in the previous forty years, the 1920–24 New York Giants and the 1942–44 St. Louis Cardinals, had won more.

Still, judging by the start of the season, there didn't seem much to worry about. The Braves, after winning their first four games in a row, shot into a good lead, which was up to four and a half games by late May. At that pace they could have come close to clinching the race by midseason, but they couldn't keep up that pace. They sputtered and stumbled and stalled and slumped, and pretty soon were in a dogfight with the San Francisco Giants, the Los Angeles Dodgers, and the Pittsburgh Pirates. Still, by the All-Star Game, they were clinging to a two-point lead over the Giants and a half-game lead over the Dodgers after having been out of first place only eight days during the entire first half of the season.

But the pennant race in the first two months was nowhere nearly as exciting as Henry Aaron's batting average. Ever since his rookie season of 1954 he had been considered a potential .400 hitter if, indeed, baseball had such a person. The last had been Ted Williams of the 1941 Boston Red Sox. In 1959 Aaron got off to such a remarkable start that even some veteran observers were sure he would crash the .400 barrier.

He was actually over .500 for three weeks and didn't drop below .400 until June 15. Even after that he continued to threaten the .400 figure, although he never again quite made it.

Usually a slow starter, Aaron began pounding the

ball on opening day, April 10, when the Braves played at Pittsburgh. He didn't stop pounding it for weeks. At Pittsburgh on opening day he had two doubles and a single. The day after, he personally beat the Pirates, tying the game with a home run in the third inning and winning it with a single in the fifth.

The Braves' home opener was with the Phillies. To the delight of a full house of rabid fans, Aaron helped win the ball game with three singles, scoring the winning run himself in the tenth inning. In each of the next two days he had a double and a single. Then, in the first game the Braves lost, to Pittsburgh by an 11–5 score, Aaron accounted for all of his team's runs with a single and a three-run homer.

When Henry beat the Reds with a single, a double, and a triple on April 21, he had an awesome collection of statistics to show for seven games—17 hits, including 5 doubles, a triple and 2 homers, 7 runs batted in, and a batting average of .567. In not one of those games had he failed to get at least 2 hits.

Robin Roberts of the Phillies finally stopped him at Philadelphia on April 22, but the next day he started all over again. That time his double and single beat Ray Semproch of the Phillies, and it was nearly a month before anyone shut him out again.

For Henry Aaron went off on a 22-game hitting streak, a streak which had everyone in baseball stopping to gape at his record every day. It positively glittered—three hits and two RBI's on April 24 at Cincinnati; another hit there the next day; a single, a double, and a homer there the day after that.

On April 29, when Aaron had a home run and three

So Near and Yet So Far

singles against the Cardinals at Milwaukee, he had piled up a fantastic .526 average in 13 games. His sixth homer of the season in the fourth inning gave Spahn a 1–0 victory the next day. In the game that followed, his single knocked in two runs and helped beat the Giants.

May 1 was his first day below .500. The whole baseball world was buzzing, "Aaron . . . Aaron . . . Aaron . . . Aaron," and the whole baseball world was wondering if he really could make it to .400 for the season.

The figuring filberts had a field day. When somebody doped out on May 16 that Aaron could go his next 53 times up without a hit and still be batting .333, Aaron was asked what he thought about that.

"I'm not thinking about anything except getting base hits," Henry said. "I'm just going after pitches. I'm not waiting, and I'm not getting behind pitchers. That puts the burden on them, not me."

Wherever he went, people wanted to know if he thought he could hit .400. It was a natural question, but a tough one to answer. Aaron, fully aware that nobody could presuppose a .400 season for a ballplayer, had a logical reply.

"Maybe I can hit .400," he said. "I've got to hold my own to the All-Star Game. I've got to avoid slumps. And I've got to get at least two hits a day to stay even."

Rogers Hornsby, holder of the modern hitting record of .424, was then batting coach of the Chicago Cubs. When asked his opinion of Aaron's chances of hitting .400, Hornsby said, "He has all the tools to do it and he's off to a wonderful start. I would say he has as good a chance as any active player, maybe as good a chance as any big-league ballplayer will ever have."

Managers lived to regret playing percentages and treating Aaron like an ordinary mortal. Once, during his hitting streak, the Braves had men on second and third with one out in the ninth inning of a 1–1 tie with Cincinnati. Manager Mayo Smith of the Reds ordered his pitcher to walk the weak-hitting Johnny O'Brien to fill the bases; this meant pitching to Eddie Mathews and Henry Aaron, but with a play at every base. When Mathews fouled out, it appeared that Smith might get away with his daring strategy. Then Aaron ruined it with a base hit that won the game. It was the only time all year any manager, including Smith, walked anyone to get to Aaron.

One day a nationally known sports columnist went to Aaron and said, "Henry, you can't hit .400. Nobody can in this day and age. What's your real ambition?"

Henry grinned and said. "Well, I have nine hundred and ninety-eight hits. I'd like to get two more so I'll have a thousand. Then I'll only be two thousand behind Musial."

During his 22-game hitting streak he had 5 games with three hits and one with four. On May 5 he doubled in the seventh to drive in the tying run against the Dodgers in Milwaukee, then doubled again in the sixteenth to drive Mathews home with the winning run in one of the longest games of the year. Nothing stopped him in the next two weeks except a slight injury that kept him out of one game. On the twelfth he jammed his ankle in Chicago, but he still collected two singles. After sitting out the next game, at St. Louis, he picked up right where he had left off. He banged out two doubles and a single and drove in three runs as the Braves beat the Cardinals, 8–7, on May 14.

He hit his ninth and tenth homers of the year in Los Angeles on the sixteenth and he belted another there the next day. Then the Braves went on to San Francisco, where Aaron had a double on May 18. That was the 22d consecutive game in which he had hit safely.

Three Giants pitchers, Jack Sanford, Joe Shipley, and Dom Zanni, finally stopped him at Candlestick Park on May 19, when Aaron failed to get a hit in four tries. But up to then, his hitting had been almost unbelievable.

From the beginning of the season to May 18, he had 61 hits in 128 times at bat for a .471 average. Among his hits were 14 doubles, 2 triples and 11 home runs, and he drove in 35 runs. He hit safely in 29 of the first 30 games he played, was personally responsible for 7 of the Braves' victories, and helped put them 3½ games in front of the pack.

His pace was, of course, impossible to maintain, and nobody could have kept it up. Yet it was nearly a month before he fell below .400. And wherever he went, he was approached by strangers asking for his autograph or simply wanting to shake his hand.

During the top of his streak he wouldn't even go to the movies for fear of jeopardizing his eyesight. In fact, one day he commented, "I haven't seen a movie this whole trip. Sure miss it."

He never lost his cool or his subtle sense of humor. One day a stranger said, "Aren't you Hank Aaron?"

"I'm Aaron," Henry said laconically.

"Well, don't be modest," the other said. "After all, you're hitting .400."

"If I were hitting .200, I'd still be Aaron," Henry said.

A week after Aaron's streak ended, the Braves were involved in one of the most amazing big-league games ever played. On the night of May 26, in Milwaukee, Harvey Haddix of the Pirates pitched twelve perfect innings against them, yet lost in the thirteenth.

It was a historic—and frustrating—performance by Haddix. The wiry 160-pounder set down thirty-six men in order. No pitcher had ever before gone more than nine perfect innings, and none had ever pitched hitless ball for more than ten and two-thirds. The Braves never came close to getting on base in the first twelve innings, although both Del Rice and Eddie Mathews sent Bill Virdon back to the center-field fence for long drives in the tenth.

While Haddix was spinning his classic, Lew Burdette was throwing a 12-hit shutout. The Pirates twice had good chances to beat Burdette. In the third they had 3 straight hits, but one base runner was thrown out trying to go from first base to third. And with one out in the tenth, pinch hitter Dick Stuart missed a home run by a whisker when Andy Pafko, playing center field, made a great catch of his long drive.

Even the 19,194 Milwaukee fans who saw the

So Near and Yet So Far

game were rooting for Haddix as he went inning after inning without allowing a man to reach first. From the ninth on, he received a standing ovation after every inning.

The game ended in the thirteenth inning on a confusing note because Henry Aaron didn't realize that a long smash by Joe Adcock had left the ball park for a home run. Felix Mantilla led off with a grounder to Don Hoak at third and was safe when Hoak's low throw pulled Rocky Nelson, the first baseman, off the bag. The error, although it finished Haddix's perfect job, kept his no-hitter alive. Mathews sacrificed, and Aaron was intentionally walked to set up a possible double play.

That brought Adcock up with two men on and one out. The big Braves' first baseman, who had fanned twice and grounded out his other two times up, smashed a towering drive which barely dropped over the wire fence in left center 375 feet from the plate.

Mantilla scored easily, and Aaron and Adcock should also have scored. But both Aaron and the umpires thought the ball had dropped inside the playing field. After touching second base to stop a force play, Henry headed for the dugout, since the winning run was already in. In the meantime, Adcock, running with his head down and not knowing which side of the fence the ball had landed on, kept going around the bases.

Manager Fred Haney and the coaches waved him back after he crossed second base and sent Aaron back to second so that he would be ahead of Adcock. Then both **jogged around** the bases, with Aaron crossing the plate first in order for Adcock to get credit for his home run. But it was too late. The damage had already been done.

Aaron, Adcock, and the umpires all pulled boners. Aaron shouldn't have taken it for granted that the ball was still in play. Adcock should have watched where he was going so as not to pass the point where Aaron had left the base paths. And the umpires should have checked with Virdon, the only one who knew that the ball had gone over the fence. Since the Pirates had lost the game anyhow when Mantilla scored, Virdon had nothing to lose admitting the ball was a home run; he later did so.

The umpires devised an impossible ruling. They gave Adcock credit for a double and Aaron credit for the run he apparently scored. If Adcock had a double, Aaron's run couldn't count, since Mantilla's would have been the winning run. If Adcock had a home run, all three runs should have counted. But that night it was called a 2–0 victory for the Braves.

The next day Warren Giles, president of the National League, set the record straight. He ruled that Adcock had only a double, because Adcock had passed Aaron on the bases, and that Mantilla's run was the only one that counted.

Confusing as the score was, there was no doubt of the result. Poor Harvey Haddix lost the most glittering pitching performance the major leagues had ever seen. His twelve innings of perfection and his twelve and a third innings of no-hit ball, although gems for the record book, added up to just another lost ball game for him.

So Near and Yet So Far

When Aaron, at the age of twenty-five, collected his thousandth hit, a single off Sandy Koufax of the Dodgers, he became the second youngest ballplayer in big-league history to reach that milestone. Only Ty Cobb of the Tigers, who had his thousandth hit at twenty-four, had been younger.

Nearing the first of two All-Star Games played that year, Aaron had three homers in one game for the first time in his career. It was particularly satisfying to him because he did it in San Francisco, where his twenty-two-game hitting streak had been stopped a month earlier.

Immediately after the first All-Star Game, the Giants moved into the lead, and they held it all but two days for the next ten weeks. In late July the Pirates knocked themselves out of the pennant race with a losing stretch of 15 out of 18 games.

That left the Braves, the Giants, and the Dodgers, but the Braves nearly killed their chances by dropping 7 in a row. They came back with 12 wins in their next 15 games. Then, in early September, they lost a crucial game to the Giants that would have put them in easy reach of the top, and that pushed them 4 behind with only 20 games to go.

If the Braves had curled over and quit at that point, nobody would have been surprised. For even though they had been almost prohibitive favorites at the beginning of the season, they had been faced with almost constant problems. In fact, if it had not been for Henry Aaron and Eddie Mathews, they would have dropped out of the race long before.

Aaron's hitting continued to be effective all year.

Although his bid to stay within range of the .400 mark didn't last, he maintained a pace of .350 or better right up to the end. The most dangerous hitter in the National League, he rarely was shut out at the plate two games in succession, more often putting together hitting streaks of ten or a dozen games.

But he and Mathews were the only consistent hitters on the ball club. Mathews was the best slugger in the league, Aaron not only a slugger but the best hitter for average. However, when they were the only men hitting well, the Braves were in trouble.

Spahn and Burdette were the only pitchers they could depend on. And the hole left at second base by Schoendienst's absence looked bigger and bigger with each passing day. Before the season ended, Haney had used eight men at second, including Schoendienst himself, who was reactivated in the last month of the season. But this was more a token than a practical gesture. Schoendienst, still weak and unable to appear more than a few innings here and there, was mostly an inspirational factor.

After the Braves lost that key game to the Giants and limped off 4 games behind with but 20 to go, the experts forgot about them and concentrated their attention on what appeared to be a two-team fight between the Dodgers and the Giants for the National League pennant.

But the problems that had kept the Braves down in the second half of the season—complacency, shaky pitching, the absence of Schoendienst, too many slumps by too many regulars—suddenly disappeared. Although he couldn't play much, Schoendienst helped simply by being there. The hitters took a new lease on life, lending Aaron and Mathews badly needed assistance at the plate. Spahn and Burdette got backing from other pitchers, especially Bob Buhl. Haney did a masterful job from the dugout.

After the defeat by San Francisco, the Braves refused to stay dead. Instead of fading out of the pennant race, as the experts expected, they injected themselves back into it by winning seven straight games. When they went west on September 14, they had made the race a three-team scramble again. On that date only one game separated the Braves, the Giants, and the Dodgers.

The Braves split one series in Los Angeles, another in San Francisco. With the race so close, a two-game winning streak could change the standings. The Giants had one, and on the morning of the nineteenth, eight days before the end of the season, they were two in front, with the Braves and the Dodgers tied for second place.

But that day the Dodgers beat the Giants in a doubleheader, and by evening those two were tied at the top, with the Braves half a game behind.

Now the league lead was changing almost every day. On September 20 the Dodgers beat the Giants again and moved up front, half a game ahead of the Braves and a game ahead of the Giants. On the twenty-first the Braves won while the others were idle, putting them into a top tie with the Dodgers and leaving the Giants a game behind.

Then the Braves took over the lead alone by winning while the other two lost, but on the twenty-third they were back in a tie with the Dodgers again, with the Giants two behind. While the Braves and Dodgers stayed on top, the Giants managed to keep their flickering hopes alive until the last day of the season, Sunday, September 26.

That morning the Braves and Dodgers were tied at the top with the Giants a game behind, and mathematically minded fans had a field day. For with all three teams in contention, there was an outside possibility of a three-way tie because the Giants had a doubleheader at St. Louis with the others playing single games. If the Giants could sweep while the Braves and Dodgers lost, a triple tie would result.

That contingency died quickly. The Giants lost the first game (they eventually lost the second, too), knocking them out. But both the Braves and the Dodgers won, leaving them in a tie and forcing the third play-off in National League history.

Baseball play-offs are among the most pressure-packed events in sports. The outcome of the pennant race is the most important factor, but not the only one. Because October weather is often unpredictable in most sections of the country, there is pressure to start the World Series on time; that means no days off between play-off games. A third problem in the case of the 1959 play-offs was the long distance between the cities involved. The teams had to travel the 2,000 miles from Milwaukee to Los Angeles without losing a day of baseball.

The play-offs opened in Milwaukee on the day after the regular season ended, with the second game and the third, if necessary, scheduled for Los Angeles.

So Near and Yet So Far

Since both clubs had used up their ace pitchers in the last couple of days of the wild pennant race, both had to start second-line pitchers in the opening play-off game on Monday, September 28. The Dodgers' starter was Danny McDevitt, with a record of 10 wins and 8 losses. On the mound for the Braves was Carlton Willey, with a mediocre 5 and 9 mark for the regular season.

It was raining hard enough in Milwaukee to delay the start of the game for forty-seven minutes, in itself enough to scratch jumpy nerves raw. The rain hurt the Braves because, instead of the County Stadium capacity of more than 48,000, it kept the friendly crowd down to less than 19,000.

The Dodgers scored a run in the first inning on two singles and an infield out. In the Braves' second, Logan walked and scored on hits by Crandall and Bruton. When McDevitt threw two called balls at Willey, he was pulled out, to be replaced by Larry Sherry, a rookie who had won six games and lost two in relief after the Dodgers brought him up from the minors on July 4.

The Braves scored again before Sherry could retire them, but it wasn't his fault. Willey reached first on Maury Wills' error to fill the bases, and Crandall scored from third on a force play, giving the Braves a 2–1 lead.

But the Dodgers tied it up in their third on three singles and went ahead, 3–2, on John Roseboro's sixth-inning home run. And that was the way it ended, as the twenty-four-year-old Sherry shut out the Braves the rest of the way. Henry Aaron, who failed to hit but walked twice, was one of Sherry's four strikeout victims.

The teams flew to Los Angeles immediately after the game and met again the next day in the Coliseum, a lopsided ball park with a short but very high fence in left and a long one in right. This time two top performers, Don Drysdale of the Dodgers and Lew Burdette of the Braves, were the starting pitchers before a disappointing crowd of fewer than 37,000 fans.

The Braves took a quick early lead when Mathews walked and Aaron doubled him to third, with both scoring on Frank Torre's single. The Dodgers got one run back in the first; then, in the second, the Braves scored again on two hits and an error, which gave them a 3–1 lead. When Charlie Neal of the Dodgers hit a homer in the fourth and Eddie Mathews smashed one in the fifth, it was 4–2 Braves.

Although the Dodgers didn't score in the seventh, they hurt the Braves badly when Norm Larker crashed into Johnny Logan at second base, knocking him out of action. With Logan on the shelf, Felix Mantilla, the starting second baseman, moved over to short, and Bobby Avila replaced him at second.

The Braves added one more run in the eighth on Crandall's triple and Mantilla's sacrifice fly, giving them what appeared to be a safe 5–2 lead going into the ninth. But Burdette, who hadn't allowed a Dodger to get past first base since Neal's homer, suddenly lost his stuff. After three straight singles filled the bases with nobody out, he was replaced by Don McMahon.

McMahon was in just long enough to give up a two-run single to Larker. With Gil Hodges on third,

So Near and Yet So Far

Carl Furillo up, and the score now 5–4, Warren Spahn came in after only two days' rest. He got the Dodgers out, but not before Furillo's sacrifice fly scored Hodges with the tying run and sent the game into extra innings.

It was still tied when Bob Rush, the fifth Braves' pitcher, walked Hodges with two out in the Dodgers' twelfth. Hodges went to second on Joe Pignatano's single; then came the break of the game.

Furillo hit a high, twisting bounder which Mantilla took behind second base. His off-balance throw to first took a crazy hop as it pulled Frank Torre off the bag, and Hodges raced home with the run that won the pennant for the Dodgers. From that day to this, observers have wondered what would have happened if Johnny Logan had been at short to make that play.

Unlike the previous day, when he had failed to get a hit, Henry Aaron had a double and a single in four official times up. Actually, he was on base four times, since he walked twice.

Except for the unhappy result of the play-offs, it was a great season for him. He won his second National League batting title with a .355 average, and he also led the league in hits, total bases, and slugging percentage. He was third in home runs, behind Mathews and Ernie Banks of the Cubs, and third in RBI's, behind Banks and Frank Robinson of the Reds.

So Henry Aaron's sixth season in the majors was one of his best as, now an established superstar, he moved steadily along the road toward baseball's Hall of Fame.

9 Steps Toward Immortality

FRED HANEY resigned as manager of the Braves right after the 1959 season ended and was replaced by the veteran Charlie Dressen, a hard-bitten old-timer and a tough disciplinarian.

There was an important front-office change, too. Johnny McHale became the general manager, succeeding John Quinn, who resigned to become general manager of the Phillies. Already in the front office as executive vice-president was Birdie Tebbetts, former Reds' manager.

All this meant little to Henry Aaron except that he had new people to deal with when negotiating his salary. Now around the $60,000 figure, Aaron had no serious salary worries. On that subject, he came out with one of the funniest remarks of the winter.

While speaking at the annual Dapper Dan dinner in Pittsburgh, he told the audience he had to catch an early plane to Milwaukee.

"I have to talk about my nineteen sixty contract before Spahn gets there and takes all the money," he said.

During the winter there was so much talk about the second-base problem that Aaron was drawn into it. Red Schoendienst, although fully recovered from his siege with tuberculosis, was thirty-seven years old and obviously nearing the end of the line. The Braves were going to need help at his position, and Dressen talked as if some of it might have to come from Aaron.

Although he had played second in the minors and for a few games in 1955, Aaron had little interest in the job.

"I'll go to second if Dressen insists," he said, "but I don't look forward to it. All I ask is that he start me there in the spring if he intends to play me there. I don't want to go there in midseason and make a fool of myself."

Aaron's reluctance was understandable. He described second base as "the most dangerous position on the field" because runners were always coming at the second baseman from behind. But that didn't bother him nearly as much as the fact that he hadn't played second for five years.

He really didn't have to worry. Dressen had no intention of trying to transform a happy outfielder into an unhappy infielder. As it turned out, he asked Aaron to fill in at second only for a couple of innings all season. Schoendienst and Les Cottier shared the job most of the time.

The 1960 season started well enough for the Braves. On opening day Aaron helped stop Roy Face, who had won 18 and lost only 1 for the Pirates in 1959, when he beat out a hit with the score 2-2 in the eighth. A minute later he scored on Joe Adcock's home run.

Two nights after that, Aaron and Adcock hit back-to-back home runs in the first inning to set the Braves up for an easy victory at Philadelphia. Henry also had two singles and a triple as he drove in four runs that night.

Later in the season he beat Don Drysdale of the Dodgers with two home runs. In those days Drysdale had trouble controlling one of the hottest tempers in baseball. When Aaron came up after hitting the first home run, Drysdale was so mad he threw three straight pitches at Henry, then walked him. On his next time up, Aaron hit his second homer on Drysdale's first pitch.

"He didn't bother me any," Henry said afterward. "I just wish I could face him with the bases full. It's his mistake when he gets mad. When he's that way, he can't beat anyone."

Despite successes here and there, the Braves got off to a miserable start in 1960. By late May they had lost as many games as they had won and were in fourth place, six and a half games off the pace set by the pennant-bound Pirates.

Although Aaron and his heavy-hitting mates, Mathews and Adcock, were piling up an impressive total of home runs, they were not hitting for average. Henry, in fact, couldn't get up over .300 and never did that year. It was the first time since his rookie year that he failed to make it.

Both he and opposing pitchers were learning that he

was human, after all. For one of the few times in his career, he had consistent trouble against right-handers. Larry Jackson of the Cardinals and Sam Jones of the Giants, both hard-throwing righties who kept the ball away from Aaron, had particularly good luck with him. Except for occasional infield hits, he did nothing against either of them.

His .292 average, which left him twelfth in the league in batting, was caused by his unusually low .271 season's mark against right-handers. Against southpaws he was as effective as ever, batting .346.

His slugging was also as dangerous as ever. He collected 40 homers, only one less than the league-leading Ernie Banks. And with Mathews and Adcock, he formed one-third of the best three-way batting punch in baseball. Mathews' 39 home runs and Adcock's 25 gave the Braves' trio a total of 104, more than the entire Phillies team and nearly as many as half the other clubs in the National League.

Aaron led the league in RBI's with 126, and his 334 total bases put him on top in that category, too. But because he failed to hit .300 and the team failed to win the pennant, he considered 1960 an off year.

"Henry Aaron," wrote Bob Wolf of the Milwaukee *Journal,* "is the only player in baseball who can hit 40 home runs and drive in 126 runs and consider it a bad year."

One teammate who marveled at him was Joe Adcock. Halfway through the season, when Aaron was down around .280 and struggling, Adcock said, "He's the greatest hitter in the game. If it weren't for night baseball, he would hit .400 every year."

Aaron blamed himself, but he was really the last man at fault. The team was weak at second base all year. Both Johnny Logan and Wes Covington had poor seasons—much poorer than Aaron's—and except for a big three pitching staff of Spahn, Burdette, and Buhl, the Braves had mound woes all year. The ageless Spahn, now thirty-nine, won 21 games and pitched a no-hitter. Burdette, who also pitched a no-hitter, won 19, and Buhl won 16. But all the rest of the staff together won only 32 games.

While the team finished second, there were definite signs that its fans were becoming disenchanted. The most obvious was the attendance. For the first time since the Braves had gone to Milwaukee in 1953, fewer than 1,500,000 people went to see them at County Stadium. It was the third straight year that attendance dropped since the peak of more than 2,200,000 in 1957.

There were other indications of disillusionment. Although the heroes were still heroes, the city was used to them. Baseball, once a plaything that made Milwaukee in its own eyes "big league," was now being taken for granted. Even winning was taken for granted. Anything less didn't count.

The fuzzy-faced kids who had taken the town by storm in 1953 were now grown men who had been through the mill. And along with the others, Henry Aaron, the most popular of all, had lost the bloom of youth. At twenty-six, he was in the prime of his career, but a twenty-six-year-old on a team that doesn't win hardly has the appeal of a twenty-three-year-old on a team that does.

When the 1960 season ended—it was the fifth one in which the Braves finished second—a new cloud loomed on the horizon. For 1961 was the first major-league expansion year. Two new teams were coming into the American League, one in Los Angeles, the other in Washington. And the old Washington franchise was moving to the Twin Cities of Minneapolis and St. Paul.

Perhaps more than anything else, this gave notice that the days of the Braves in Milwaukee might be numbered. The Twin Cities had been Braves' territory ever since 1953. The new Twins could cut sharply into the orbit of the Braves. Fans once willing to travel hundreds of miles to watch the Braves in Milwaukee now had a team of their own much closer.

But the true effect of the new Twins on the old Braves was still several years in the future. The immediate problem the Braves had as they faced the 1961 season was that the ball club which had won two pennants, barely missed two others, and hadn't finished below second place in six years no longer ranked as a serious pennant contender.

Red Schoendienst, through as a regular, was released after the 1960 season, leaving the gap at second wider than ever. Johnny Logan was also through, making shortstop a disaster area. And Del Crandall, the dependable catcher of so many years, had arm trouble.

The outfield, although not set, looked fairly good, and the pitching staff, loaded with promising young ballplayers and still spearheaded by Spahn, Burdette, and Buhl, would be in good shape if one youngster could make the starting rotation. What the Braves didn't have they hoped to pick up in trades.

Two important midwinter deals shored up the infield but weakened the outfield. In one, the Braves sent pitchers Juan Pizarro and Joey Jay to Cincinnati for shortstop Roy McMillan. In the other, they obtained second baseman Frank Bolling from Detroit for Bill Bruton.

If young outfielders who had appeared to be certain future stars had developed, everything might have been all right in 1961. But when they failed, Bruton's loss left a shambles of the outfield. Everyone was affected, and the man who felt the hardest impact was Henry Aaron.

Aaron, the best right fielder in baseball, had no desire to play anywhere else. But manager Charlie Dressen asked him to work out in center field at spring training because he thought Aaron might have to play there during the season.

"I don't want to put Henry in center field," Dressen told baseball experts before the season began. "And I won't start him there. But if our outfield doesn't shape up as well as we hope, I may be forced to move him. Let's face it. He may be our best right fielder, but he's also our best center fielder. He's got the best arm and he covers more ground than anyone else on the club."

Aaron wasn't happy at the prospect. "I don't like it," he said, "but if Dressen wants it, that's the way it will be."

Henry had signed for an estimated $65,000 salary, a substantial raise over his 1960 figure. When someone asked him if he got it on condition he would play center field, he said, "All it says in my contract is for me to play ball."

Despite all the talk, he began the season in his familiar old right-field spot. On opening day Lee Maye was in left and John DeMerit in center. Neither set the world on fire, and within two weeks Al Spangler and Wes Covington also had a crack at the outfield jobs.

On April 23 Aaron was shifted to center field. With the exception of a day here and there, Henry was the Braves' center fielder for the next two months. During that time he rarely was flanked by the same outfielders two days in a row.

Besides Maye, DeMerit, Spangler, and Covington, Felix Mantilla and Mel Roach were tried in the outfield before the end of April. The second week in May the Braves traded Roach to the Cubs for Frank Thomas and sold Covington to the White Sox. Thomas, a power hitter, moved in at left field, stabilizing that spot, but Aaron remained in center while Dressen continued to experiment in right.

In the meantime, more changes gave the Braves a new look. When Crandall's arm failed to improve, the Braves brought Joe Torre up from the minors to do the catching. Another indication of the passing of an era came in mid-June when, just before the trading deadline, the Braves sent Johnny Logan to Pittsburgh for outfielder Gino Cimoli.

Only then did Aaron get his old right-field job back. Cimoli, off to a good start, moved in at center field, and for most of the remainder of the season, the

Braves' outfield consisted of Thomas in left, Cimoli in center, and Aaron in right.

There were occasional high spots, but 1961 was not a good year for the Braves. They finished fourth behind the Reds, the Dodgers, and the Giants. They drew barely 1,100,000. It was their poorest finish and their lowest attendance since moving to Milwaukee. During the entire season the only time they looked like the old Braves was in August, when they enjoyed a 10-game winning streak.

In early June, Henry Aaron was involved in a record-breaking home-run barrage when he, Eddie Mathews, Joe Adcock, and Frank Thomas hit successive homers in the seventh inning of a losing game against the Reds. Mathews and Aaron hit theirs off Jim Maloney, the other two off Marshall Bridges, who relieved him. It was the first time any big-league club had ever hit four straight homers, although teams have done it since.

As the season progressed and it became obvious that the Braves weren't going anywhere—they were fifth most of the year—the club's morale showed signs of collapse. Dressen, never popular with his players because of his demands for strict adherence to training rules on pain of stiff fines, had disciplinary problems all year.

There were playboys on the club, but one man he never had to worry about was Henry Aaron. Always in shape, Aaron was a model of propriety both on and off the field. He kept sensible hours, neither drank nor smoked, and concerned himself only with the business of playing ball.

"If everyone were like Aaron, I wouldn't collect a dime in fines," Dressen once said. "I'd like to have a whole ball club of Aarons."

Not having a whole ball club of Aarons, Dressen lost his job in September. The Braves looked only to their front office for a successor, naming Birdie Tebbetts to run the team on the field. It was too late for anyone to help. Tebbetts let the club play out the year while he planned for 1962.

Although Aaron got back up into the .300's in batting, he failed to lead the league in any important category except doubles, of which he had 39. His .327 average left him fifth, his 120 RBI's left him fourth, and his 34 home runs gave him sixth place among the league's sluggers.

For him, the season was hardly a total loss, however. Besides adding substantially to his records, he moved another step closer to baseball immortality. In eight years of major-league play he now had 253 home runs and a lifetime batting average of .319. The only man ahead of him in batting among players with 1,000 or more games was Stan Musial.

Musial was nearing the finish of his career. Henry Aaron was only twenty-seven years old. Barring illness or injury, he still had many years of greatness ahead.

10 Triple Crown Near Miss

SINCE THE END of the Braves' glory days, a pattern had formed—Henry Aaron continued to star while the ball club continued to slip. This didn't change in 1962. Under Birdie Tebbetts the Braves had no more luck than they had had under Charlie Dressen. But Aaron rolled right along, playing as if he were still helping to win pennants and adding more luster to his already remarkable record.

A loner since his roommate, Billy Bruton, had been traded, Henry again had a close pal on the ball club. His brother Tommie, five and a half years younger and 20 pounds heavier than Henry, who had been in the farm system four seasons, finally made it to the Braves in 1962. Although he was later in and out of the minors until returning to the big club to stay in 1968, Tommie spent the entire 1962 season at Milwaukee, where he roomed with Henry on the road and lived with him at home.

Triple Crown Near Miss

Tommie could play both infield and outfield and could hit an occasional long ball, but he was plagued by serious batting weaknesses. Far behind his brother in natural ability, he still was able to help Henry win some ball games. He originally appeared in the lineup as a first baseman, but his first chance to start came in a way that pleased neither him nor Henry.

On April 22, Henry bruised a knee and a couple of ribs when he ran into the right-field fence going after a fly ball in Milwaukee. Tommie replaced him, and when Henry returned to the lineup, Tommie moved over to left field. From then on, Tommie swung back and forth between the outfield, first base, and the bench.

Henry got off to a poor start, aggravated by his early-season injury. But once he was back in the lineup, his hitting picked up, and soon he was up where he belonged, among the National League leaders.

He enjoyed two remarkable hitting streaks. In June he hit safely in 14 straight games, collecting 27 hits in 58 times up for a .466 batting average. In that stretch he had 7 home runs and batted in 25 runs. From then on, while maintaining an average in the .330's, his slugging was fantastic. Up through July 31 he had 29 homers, 91 RBI's, and a .332 batting mark.

On August 1, in a game against Houston at Milwaukee, he had two hits in four times up. The next time he went hitless was August 26, when Dick Ellsworth stopped him at Chicago. In between he hit safely in 25 straight games.

Unlike his earlier long streaks, when he frequently had two or three hits a game, Aaron often had to struggle along with one hit, so his average rose only a few points. But several times he came through with bombs that meant ball games, as he led the Braves through a string of 17 wins in the 25 games of his streak.

Three times he teamed up with Tommie to help the Braves win. In the second game of a doubleheader against the Phillies in Milwaukee, Henry was one of three men who scored ahead of Tommie's game-winning grand-slam home run. Ten days later both he and Tommie homered as the Braves won at Cincinnati. And six days after that he scored ahead of Tommie as the Braves beat the Giants in Milwaukee.

Because Tommie was involved, these events gave Henry particular pleasure. But there were also plenty of times in his streak when he won games by his efforts alone. He beat the Cubs in Milwaukee with his 30th home run. He beat Houston with, of all things, two stolen bases in a game in which he collected three singles. He helped blast the Giants with his 32d and 33d homers. And his 34th and 35th beat the Cubs on successive days. During the streak Aaron had 6 homers and 16 RBI's and batted .372.

Aaron did far better than the ball club, which finished fifth and drew only 766,921 fans. For the third time in his big-league career, he went over the 40 mark in home runs, finishing second to Willie Mays with 45. Only Mays and Frank Robinson had more runs batted in than Henry, who collected 128. And his .323 batting average was the fifth best in the league.

Aaron's lifetime home-run total was perhaps the most significant of all. He finished the season with 298, a figure that made it evident that he would be right up with all the great sluggers of history if he kept his health. At that time only twenty men had hit 300 or more homers. Considering his age, his power, and his condition, Aaron was almost surely headed for 500, a total reached by only a handful.

The dismal finish of 1962 cost Birdie Tebbetts his job. The Braves, desperate to find some way of beefing up their ball club, picked Bobby Bragan, a firebrand noted for a combination of toughness and original ideas, as the new manager.

Bragan was not the only innovation that year. For the first time since 1947, the Braves did not train at Bradenton. Instead, they moved into a spacious new ball park at West Palm Beach, on the east coast of Florida. So when Henry Aaron reported for spring training in 1963, it was to a new manager at a new base.

And as always, there were more new men on the ball club while more of the old ones were gone or going. Joe Adcock was traded with a pitcher to the Cleveland Indians for two young outfielders and a relief pitcher. The amazing Warren Spahn seemed as good as ever at forty-two, but the slipping Lew Burdette went to the Cardinals in May, 1963. Del Crandall had made a fine comeback in 1962. However, he, too, was obviously on his way out. He lasted through the 1963 season but spent most of it on the bench.

Of the old guard that had brought baseball supremacy to Milwaukee, only Spahn, Mathews, and Aaron were still regulars. Most of the others were newcomers.

So Henry Aaron, at twenty-nine, was already one of the ball club's elder statesmen.

In 1963 he had the worst spring training of his career. Not until the last week in Florida did he get his batting average up over .200. He ended up at .206, with one home run and six runs batted in.

The problem was not so much Aaron as the ball park. There were peculiar wind currents which he couldn't get used to, with the result that when the Braves played at home, Aaron had nothing but trouble. His batting average in West Palm Beach was actually under .200, and those who watched him all season didn't know what to think.

"He can't be through," one said. "Not Henry Aaron. But he certainly looks awful down here."

As usual, Henry refused to worry.

"What happens here doesn't count," he said. "They don't figure averages until the season begins in April."

And when the season started, he was once again sensational. In his first 14 games he batted .358, had 4 home runs and 10 RBI's, and once again proved that he was one of the great hitters of baseball.

The 299th home run of his career came on April 11 against the Mets at Milwaukee. The 300th came against them eight days later in New York. On April 22 Aaron reached two more milestones. He drove in his 1000th run with his 302d homer. The home run put him into a tie with Rogers Hornsby for nineteenth place in the all-time standing.

"What about Mel Ott's National League record of five hundred and eleven?" Aaron was asked at that point. "Do you think you can break it?"

"I'm not putting any records out of reach," Henry said. "Right now all I think about is staying healthy. If I do that, I think I can break a whole lot of records."

In the meantime, his teammate of ten years, Eddie Mathews, was adding frosting to his own cake. On April 17, Mathews hit the 400th homer of his career. A hundred homers ahead of Aaron and two years older, Mathews had a better shot at the magic 500 mark than Aaron did. However, Mathews had reached the peak of his career and was actually on the way down. Aaron's was still ahead of him.

When Henry hit the eighth grand-slam homer of his career off Lindy McDaniel in Chicago, he apologized for it. The ball landed on top of the right-field wall and bounced into the bleachers at Wrigley Field, a "wrong field" hit for the right-handed Aaron.

"I didn't hit it very good," he said. "It wouldn't have come close without the wind, but I'll take it."

By then he was leading the league in home runs and runs batted in and was fourth in batting. Now, for the first time in his career, he had a shot at the Triple Crown, one of baseball's few slugging honors he had never won.

Two months later, he and Tommie had a narrow escape when a fire broke out in their St. Louis hotel room after an air-conditioning unit blew up. Henry was eating breakfast and Tommie was lying on a bed when it happened. The two, lucky to get out alive, only lost some clothes they hadn't yet packed.

"Are you all right?" a police officer asked Henry.

"Yeah," Henry replied. "But if I go oh for four tonight, I'll say I wasn't."

That night he belted a home run and had two other hits against the Cardinals.

By the All-Star Game his Triple Crown shot seemed gone because he was eleventh in batting, although he led the league in RBI's and was second in home runs. But then his hitting picked up, and as the season moved into its final six weeks, he was in the thick of everything again.

On August 14 he settled an old score when he walloped a grand-slam home run off Don Drysdale of the Dodgers in Milwaukee. It was Aaron's second slam of the year, the ninth of his career, and it won the ball game. Up to then Drysdale had allowed only two other homers all year.

The home run was Aaron's 32d of the season; it made him the first hitter in the majors to pick up 100 RBI's and gave him a .315 batting average. Now he led in runs batted in, was second in homers and sixth in batting, so his Triple Crown hopes were still alive. If he made it, he would be the first National League winner in twenty-six years. The last had been Ducky Medwick of the Cardinals in 1937.

As the season moved into its final stages, Aaron was obviously the league's most dangerous batter, regardless of whether or not he won the Triple Crown. On the Braves' last trip into Los Angeles, he tore the Dodgers apart.

When the club left town, manager Walter Alston of the Dodgers, who were about to win the pennant, said, "We gave Aaron the works. Fed him nothing but very bad pitches, jammed him, dusted him, worked every trick to pick him off base, got rough on him when he slid.

"He ended up with two singles and a home run," Alston went on. "He stole a base. He accounted for four Braves runs. He robbed Tommy Davis of a triple with a fantastic catch. More than anyone else in the business, he makes me wish I weren't a manager."

Aaron missed the Triple Crown by seven percentage points. He led the league in RBI's with 130 and tied Willie McCovey of the Giants for the home-run championship. Each had 44, and curiously enough, each wore the number 44.

Aaron batted .319, for a third-place tie with Dick Groat of the Cardinals. The league champion, Tommy Davis, hit .326. With seven more points, Aaron could have made National League history.

When the season was over, Aaron, with tongue in cheek, insisted that he got the biggest kick out of his 31 stolen bases.

"It should have been thirty-six," he said. "I got caught five times because I looked at the catcher. I shouldn't have been caught at all."

Aaron and the forty-two-year-old Spahn, who won 23 games, enjoyed great years, but the Braves had their worst since going to Milwaukee. Sixth in a ten-club league, they landed in the second division for the first time since leaving Boston. They did show a very slight attendance rise but were still well under 800,000, and their hopes for the immediate future weren't any brighter.

Although Mathews got over the 400 mark in home runs, he had one of the poorest seasons of his career.

He hit .263 and had only 23 homers, his fewest since breaking into the majors. But Henry Aaron and Mathews were closing in on one of the most interesting and most obscure home-run records in baseball—total homers for two sluggers on the same ball club.

The National League record was 745, held by Duke Snider and Gil Hodges of the Dodgers. At the end of the 1963 season, after Aaron and Mathews had been together on the Braves ten years, they had 692 between them. Although Mathews had a personal total of 422 and was seventh in the all-time standing, while Aaron had 342 and was seventeenth, they were almost exactly even as teammates.

When Aaron joined the Braves in 1954, Mathews had already been with them two years, and his 1952 and 1953 home runs could not be counted in the total the two had as teammates. But everything counted from 1954 through 1963, when Aaron had 342 homers and Mathews 350. And as long as the two stayed together on the Braves, everything would continue to count.

It was a foregone conclusion that they would pass Snider and Hodges in a year or two, but the record they really were after was the all-time major-league mark of 838 held by Babe Ruth and Lou Gehrig. The magic of Ruth and Gehrig had been part of baseball's tradition for more than thirty years. To break their record would really mean something.

Not that Henry hadn't already left indelible marks in the record books during his ten years in the majors. He had topped .300 in eight of them. He had slammed at least 25 homers in seven, driven in at least 100 runs in nine, averaged 153 games a season, hit homers in every park in the league a record seven straight times.

He had twice led the league in batting, twice led it in homers, three times led it in runs batted in, six times led it in total bases. He had 1,121 runs batted in, the most of any active player for that ten-year stretch, and his .320 batting average was higher than anyone else's in the same period.

In ten years he had collected 740 extra-base hits, 134 more than the far more highly publicized Mickey Mantle over a longer period. He had won three Golden Gloves from the *Sporting News* as the league's outstanding right fielder, had won the Most Valuable Player award, and had played in every All-Star Game since 1955.

Teammates and opponents alike continued to marvel at both his hitting and his fielding, which was often overlooked. Gene Oliver, a catcher traded to the Braves by the Cardinals in 1963, ruefully remembered days when he and his pitcher tried to get Aaron out.

"Pitchers just don't set Henry up," Oliver said. "He sets them up."

And Ron Perranoski, who frequently had faced Aaron as a Dodger relief pitcher, said, "Aaron not only knows what the pitch will be, but where it will be."

Aaron's judgment in the outfield, his deceptive speed, and his ability to make almost any play look easy never failed to impress baseball men. One day, when a ball popped out of his glove after he had made a long run, he grabbed it with his bare hand before it hit the ground.

"If Willie Mays had made that play, everyone in

the country would have known about it," an observer said. "With Henry, nobody makes anything of it. He does things like that almost every day."

No matter how many records he broke or how great he became, Aaron continued to be so self-effacing he often went completely unnoticed.

"The thing about him is," a friend once said, "he just never does anything more newsworthy than playing ball better than anyone else in the business. He has no adjustment problems. He never loses his temper. His cap never falls off. He stays out of nightclubs. You just don't hear anything about him off the field."

People didn't even hear about the nice things Aaron did, for he would have been the last to talk about them. But he was a man of great compassion, who quietly helped others without anyone's learning about it except by accident.

For years Henry had spent a couple of weeks in the autumn shooting pheasants in Dolan, South Dakota, with Lefty Miller, a friend from the Northern League, where he had once played. But not until South Dakota State Senator Pat Keel called attention to it on the floor of the state legislature did anyone dream that Aaron never had gone there without spending some time every day at a school for mentally retarded boys in Frankfort, South Dakota.

"I don't know of any public figure who takes a stronger interest in the handicapped young than this young man from baseball," Senator Keel declared. "He has a great heart."

Aaron's patience with the mentally retarded was never better illustrated than one day when he taught a seventeen-year-old boy to throw a baseball. He worked with the boy for an hour before the youngster succeeded. Then, with vacant eyes, the boy went up to Aaron and tried to drive the ball into his face.

Aaron gently reached out, held the boy's arm, laughed, and said, "Fine. You threw it very well. We'll try again tomorrow."

And every day that he was in South Dakota that year he spent an hour or so working with the boy.

One day during the winter, Ernie Johnson, the former Braves' pitcher who had become the club's public relations director, phoned to ask Aaron to meet him at the Milwaukee Children's Hospital to visit a sick boy who had asked for Henry.

"Right away," Aaron said.

As he and Johnson walked into the ward, the youngster yelled, "There's Hank. I know him."

Aaron spent two hours with the child, who was dying of cancer. When they left, Johnson said, "So you've been here before."

"Yep," Henry said.

It was the first Johnson or anyone else in the Braves organization knew that Aaron had ever set foot in the place.

11 Milwaukee Swan Song

BY THE END of the 1963 season it was obvious that the love affair between Milwaukee and the Braves was over. The city which had supported a winner with such unprecedented enthusiasm turned its back completely on a loser. The dwindling attendance made it imperative for the ball club to look elsewhere for a home.

Not that Milwaukee couldn't have continued to support a major-league ball club. Although much of the potential market had been preempted by the Twins in the Minneapolis-St. Paul area, there was enough left to keep a team in Milwaukee. But even when they were riding high, the Braves' brass had been at constant swords' points with the city fathers and county officials.

So much animosity had been built up over the years that there was no chance of a reconciliation. If Milwaukee were to remain a big-league city, it would have to be with some other club. It was just a question of time when the Braves would leave and of selection where they would go.

First rumors that it would be Atlanta came in the summer of 1963, when stories began appearing that the Southern metropolis would get the ball club. In October the Braves, who had denied the Atlanta rumor, announced they intended to stay in Milwaukee.

In the spring of 1964 the city of Atlanta disclosed plans to construct an $18,000,000 stadium because it had a commitment from a big-league team to move there in 1965. A couple of months later the *Sporting News* broke a story that the Braves were definitely the team. Again the Braves denied the rumor, pointing out that they had a contract to stay at the Milwaukee County Stadium at least through 1965.

But now there was every indication that the Braves would be in Atlanta within a year or two. Braves' officials were constantly in and out of the city. Broad hints about what a great baseball territory Atlanta could be were dropped all over the National League. Yet throughout the 1964 season the Braves continued to deny any plans to move out of Milwaukee.

In the meantime, Milwaukee's civic leaders put on a desperate attempt to keep the Braves by promoting all sorts of attendance gimmicks. Opening day of 1964 was a sellout, and although the team did little better than it had in 1963, more fans went out to watch it than in any year since 1961. Attendance for the 1964 season climbed well over the 900,000 mark.

Then the Braves' owners, while acknowledging the sincerity of the Milwaukee fans, began talking of poor television conditions. Television had become a major source of revenue in all professional sports. Because Milwaukee was hemmed in by Lake Michigan on the east, Chicago on the south, and the Twin Cities on the north, it was not easy to sell sponsors on Milwaukee.

And while worrying about poor television prospects there, baseball people pointed out how unlimited the television possibilities were in Atlanta, where the entire Southeast would be open to the team that went there.

When the 1964 season ended, the Braves dropped any pretense of staying in Milwaukee by applying to the National League for permission to move to Atlanta in 1965. It might have been granted then except that the county of Milwaukee obtained a court order compelling the Braves to honor their 1965 commitment in Milwaukee.

So the league, unwilling to get involved in what threatened to become a messy lawsuit, gave the Braves permission to move to Atlanta in 1966, but not before. That meant the Braves would be lame ducks in Milwaukee for a year. They would play in Milwaukee while openly planning what now was a definite move to the South.

In December, 1964, they bought the Atlanta club in the International League, which gave them ownership of the territory and freedom to move the International League franchise elsewhere when they took the Braves there in 1966. The Braves then opened offices in Atlanta, and most of the club's officials, including Johnny McHale, the president and general manager, moved there before the 1965 season began. Only the ballplayers and a skeleton front-office staff stayed in Milwaukee.

The Braves thus became the first major-league team in baseball history to play in one city while organizing in another. It was a ludicrous situation. Also while there had been several franchise shifts, including that of the Braves themselves from Boston to Milwaukee, this was the first time since the early days of baseball that a big-league city had ever been left without a ball club.

The Braves were accused of having milked Milwaukee dry, then abandoning it. But because of the circumstances they had no choice. For three years they had lost money in Milwaukee, and they stood to lose considerably more. The only way they could make it back would be to move. And since they had been offered a lush television contract and would be the first major-league team in the South, Atlanta was a logical place for them to go.

It was hard to evaluate just what effect the rumors and the eventual decision to move had on the ballplayers. In general, professional ballplayers don't care where they play because most of them don't live in the city they play in anyhow. But to those who do, a move elsewhere can be a shattering experience.

Henry Aaron and his family had been living in Milwaukee for several years. In 1959 they settled down in a spacious new home in the suburb of Mequon, an upper-middle-class community about 20 miles northeast of the County Stadium. The house, built of stone and redwood, was a split-level, with two stories at one end and one at the other.

Off a huge living room was a patio built in the shape of a baseball field with a brick wall around it and "bullpen" benches in the "outfield" and a barbecue pit in the equivalent of dead center field. On each side of a stone fireplace in the living room were trophy cases, both full of awards Aaron had won since joining the Braves.

Aside from the fact that he had such a comfortable home, Henry liked the life of a country squire. He and his wife had plenty of friends in Milwaukee, they enjoyed the respect of their neighbors—most of whom were white—and they had no desire to leave.

They were particularly reluctant to return to the South. Both had grown up there, Henry in Mobile, Barbara in Jacksonville, and neither wanted their children to grow up there. Despite all this, there would be compensations in moving to Atlanta. It was the most liberal city in the South, perhaps the only big city where a black family could be as happy as in any city in the North. And there was always the problem of Larry, their second son.

Larry was asthmatic. He could not stand the rugged Milwaukee winters, during which he lived with his grandparents in Mobile. If the family went to Atlanta to live, he could be with them all the year round. This was a big enough plus to make up for all the possible disadvantages.

While talk of moving seemed more important than anything else, the Braves still had ball games to play. There was one important change as they opened the 1964 season. During the winter Del Crandall and two pitchers had been traded to the Giants for Felipe Alou and three other ballplayers. Crandall's departure was another lost link with the past. Now only Spahn, Mathews, and Aaron were left.

The Braves team which manager Bobby Bragan took North had several men who could play more than one position. Alou and Lee Maye could play first or the outfield. Joe Torre and Gene Oliver could catch and play first. Dennis Menke, the shortstop, could play any infield position.

The most promising rookie was a shy young outfielder from the Dominican Republic named Rico Carty. When Aaron, whose brother was back in the minors, heard that Bragan preferred rooming someone with Carty who would help the youngster learn English, Henry volunteered.

Bragan went to Carty and, with Alou, another Dominican, interpreting, said, "How would you like to room with Number 44?" Carty's eyes widened.

"Why would he want me?" he said.

"He asked for you," Bragan said.

Carty never forgot Aaron's kind gesture. Years later he said, "I was just a scared kid from another country, and he was one of the big stars of the team, but he treated me as an equal. He helped me learn English, and he helped me learn baseball the big-league way. Rooming with him that spring was the greatest thing that ever happened to me."

The Braves got off to a terrible start, partly because they couldn't get a set lineup and partly because of pitching problems. Too much versatility did more harm than good. Torre and Oliver never knew whether they would catch or play first. Menke was all over the infield. Alou and Maye, both outfielders, occasionally were brought in to play first. While Bragan was responsible for all the shifting around, he could hardly be blamed for trying to find a winning combination. The trouble was that his switches were unexpected and sometimes resented.

His troubles were compounded by injuries. When Alou suffered torn knee cartilages in June, he was crippled for the rest of the year, although he played much of it. Carty replaced him in the outfield and did a remarkable job, both at bat and in the field. His .330 average was second in the National League only to the batting champion, Bob Clemente of the Pirates.

When Frank Bolling was hurt, Bragan unexpectedly put Aaron at second, a position Henry hated. He played only eleven games there; then Bragan sent him back to the outfield, filling in at second with Mike de la Hoz and Bill Woodward until Bolling returned. It was the last time Aaron ever played second base.

The Braves' pitching problem was aggravated by the sudden collapse of Warren Spahn. The ageless lefthander, after seventeen marvelous years, finally lost his master's touch. The year before, at forty-two, he had won 23 games. Now he could win only 6. This, of course, should have been no surprise, but he had been so great for so long that even he thought he could go on forever. Thirteen times a 20-game winner, seventeen times a 100-man strikeout artist, pitcher of two no-hitters, one five days after his fortieth birthday, holder of many major-league records for southpaws, he had been the big man of the Braves' pitching staff since 1947.

Now somebody else had to be the big man, and it

took time for the others to realize this fact. Eventually, Tony Cloninger, who won 19 games, and Denny Lemaster, who won 17, pulled up the slack, but it took both nearly half the season to get started. In the meantime, the ball club sputtered along so badly that as late as June 21 it was in ninth place. From there, the only way the Braves could go was up, but they never got into a winning groove until after the All-Star Game.

Aaron himself sputtered for a long time before he caught fire. Although he managed to keep above .300, he didn't begin really swinging the bat until midseason. And from the All-Star Game on, he was as dangerous as anyone in the league.

The Braves did well during the second half of the season, but they had so much ground to make up they were never in the pennant race. Still, except for the St. Louis Cardinals, who won the flag, they were the hottest team in the National League during the last two months of the season.

The 1964 National League race is remembered today as the year the Phillies folded. After leading the league all season and going into September 10 games in front, the Phillies lost 10 in a row, putting the pennant within reach of three other clubs. By the next to the last day of the season the Giants, Phillies, Reds, and Cardinals all had a shot at the flag, and only the Giants were out of the race on the morning of the last day.

While baseball fans remember that the season ended with the Cardinals on top and the Reds, Phillies, and Giants right at their heels, few are still aware that the Braves were the closest fifth-place team in history. Fourteen games out on September 15, they won 10 of their last 11 and finished only 5 behind the Cardinals. If the race had lasted another week, they might have won it at the rate they were going.

Just how good a fifth-place team they were could be shown by the fact they won 88 games, as many as the pennant-winning Dodgers of 1959 and the second-place Braves of 1960. And despite everyone's slow start, they ended up the hardest-hitting team in the league, leading it in batting, runs, and total bases and finishing second only to the Giants in home runs.

They had four .300 hitters, with Carty second at .330, Aaron third at .328, Torre fourth at .321, and Maye eleventh at .304. They also had five men—Aaron, Mathews, Carty, Menke, and Torre—with 20 or more home runs. Henry's total of 24 was his lowest since 1954, and Mathews' 23-homer year was marred by his anemic .233 batting average.

But Aaron and Mathews were closing in on the National League home-run record for two men on the same club. By the end of the 1964 season they had 739, only 6 short of the mark shared by Gil Hodges and Duke Snider of the Dodgers.

Aaron reached a milestone on July 12, when he collected his 2,000th hit. This still left him well behind Stan Musial, but Musial had retired in 1963 with 3,630, a mark that could be within Aaron's reach before he finished his career. Henry, who had once kidded about the long gap between his totals and Musial's, was moving up on the great Cardinals' slugger.

Although the season was not Aaron's best, it might have been very close to it if Henry hadn't suffered a painful ankle injury at Cincinnati the first week of September. It came at a time when he was murdering the ball, and although it kept him out of action for only a few days, it hampered him for the rest of the season.

Yet he continued to help the ball club. He had a seven-game hitting streak during the last week of September, when the Braves were the hottest club in baseball. They won all seven games, with Aaron either scoring or driving in at least one run in each.

But at the end of the 1964 season he had too much on his mind to worry about personal honors. His ankle had not healed. He wasn't sure whether or not to move his family to Atlanta. And he and his teammates faced a lame-duck season in Milwaukee which was sure to be painful for everyone.

Two months after the 1964 season ended, another link to the glorious Braves' past in Milwaukee was broken when Warren Spahn went to the New York Mets. Now only Aaron and Mathews were left as living monuments to the happy days of the mid-fifties.

Aaron spent the winter around Milwaukee, working with his old teammate Bill Bruton, with whom he had been involved in various business enterprises for years, resting at his Mequon home, occasionally attending banquets or keeping speaking engagements. The family also made a couple of trips to Mobile while wrestling with the problem of whether or not to move South.

Of more immediate concern was the condition of Aaron's ankle. As the weeks and months rolled by without any signs of improvement, it became increasingly evident that an operation would probably be necessary. Calcification had formed in some of the tendons, causing periodic pain which never completely disappeared. Doctors had some hope that it might be broken up by proper exercise, but this became slimmer as time passed.

There was still no marked improvement when Aaron reported for spring training in Florida. He worked hard, hoping that might be the answer to his ankle problem, but it wasn't. Instead of getting better, the ankle got worse. Although doctors now wanted to operate, Henry insisted on continuing to work out, in the hope something would happen which would make surgery unnecessary.

Nothing did. Aaron played in a couple of exhibition games and even hit a homer in one, but his ankle continued to plague him. He finally submitted to an operation on March 17 and missed the rest of spring training and the first three weeks of the regular season.

Without him the Braves got off to a miserable start. Booed at home and strangers on the road, they had nothing to keep them going except their pride. By the time Aaron rejoined them in late April they were in ninth place and Milwaukee fans were staying away from the ball park in droves. The Braves were there only physically. All their executives except Don Davidson, the traveling secretary, had already moved to Atlanta, where a new stadium and new fans were waiting to embrace them in 1966. In the meantime, they played out their 1965 schedule before poor crowds and gaping sections of empty seats.

Things got better when Aaron came back. Although he wasn't quite himself, he hit well almost from the start. He made a couple of pinch-hitting appearances, then got back into the regular lineup on April 27. Although rusty from his long layoff, he hit two of the most important home runs of his career within five days. They helped make him and Mathews the greatest one-two punch in the history of the National League.

The first, off Ron Taylor of the Cardinals on April 29, was the 744th Aaron and Mathews had hit as Braves teammates. That took them to within one of the mark held by Hodges and Snider. The next day Mathews hit one off Ray Herbert of the Phillies, tying the Dodger pair.

Then, on May 2, Aaron hit the homer that broke the record, a long shot off Bo Belinsky of the Phillies in the second game of a doubleheader in Milwaukee. That was number 746. Now, not too far away, was the all-time mark of 793, shared by Babe Ruth and Lou Gehrig.

Oddly enough, the figuring filberts were unaware of this record. Although one of the most interesting of all baseball marks, it was not pinpointed exactly because everyone was sure that Ruth and Gehrig had a much higher total. After all, Ruth's career mark of 714 and Gehrig's of 494 added up to a figure out of sight of Aaron and Mathews.

But they all didn't count. Ruth was hitting homers in quantity between 1919 and 1924 before Gehrig made it to the majors. He and Ruth were together only through 1934. Ruth was with the Boston Braves in the early part of the 1935 season before he retired from baseball, while Gehrig continued to hit plenty of home runs for the Yankees until illness forced him out of baseball in 1939.

So it wasn't unusual or unlikely that neither Aaron nor Mathews nor close observers of the game would be aware that the combined home-run total of the famous Yankee sluggers was actually within such easy range that the Braves' pair could reach it before the 1965 season ended.

When Aaron hit his 27th homer of the season off Tracy Stallard of the Cardinals at St. Louis on August 17, it went unnoticed. But this happened to be the 793d homer for Aaron and Mathews together, and it tied the total for Ruth and Gehrig as Yankee teammates.

Three days later Mathews hit his 29th homer of the year off Don Cardwell of the Pirates. That was the 794th homer which set a new record for two teammates. But it wasn't spotted until Aaron hit 2 homers off Juan Marichal of the Giants in Milwaukee on September 17. This put him and Mathews over the 800 mark and inspired Bob Wolf of the Milwaukee *Journal* to check up on the home-run record of Ruth and Gehrig as teammates. And that was the first time the baseball world realized that Aaron and Mathews had already broken it.

In the meantime, the Braves blew hot and cold all year. They made a good recovery after Aaron joined them, moved up into contention in June, then nose-dived all the way to fifth place when they lost 16 out of 23 games. But after the All-Star Game they won 10 in succession to struggle back into the pennant race, where they remained most of August. At one point they took 11 of 13 games and for two days were in

Milwaukee Swan Song

first place, but in the last week of August they lost 8 out of 10 and slipped down again.

Yet they still weren't out of it until mid-September. On the first they were only 2 games behind the league-leading Dodgers and as late as the twelfth they were in fourth place but just 2½ games out. Then they folded, losing 14 of their last 21 games and finishing fifth.

Aaron had a typical year. Even though he hit .355 in his first 10 games, he complained that he didn't feel right at the plate and that the operation had set him back too far to permit him to have a decent year. His first time in Houston's Astrodome in late May, he had a single, a double, and a home run, but he pooh-poohed the performance.

"You can't go by that," he said. "The pitcher was Larry Dierker, an eighteen-year-old who threw nothing but fast balls and curves. He threw me only one change. Against older guys I might be lost again."

But he wasn't lost. On the contrary, he got better as the season progressed, ending up with a .318 batting average, 32 home runs, and 89 RBI's. He was second in the league in batting only to Bob Clemente of the Pirates, who won his second straight title, and well up among the leaders in other departments.

In their final season at Milwaukee, the Braves drew a record low crowd of less than 556,000. The people who stayed away missed watching one of the hardest-hitting ball clubs of modern times. No fewer than six Braves, Aaron, Mathews, Alou, Torre, Mack Jones, and Gene Oliver, hit 20 or more home runs, a major-league record. Three, Aaron, Mathews and Jones, had over 30.

Henry's 32 homers gave him a career total of 398 and exactly 100 for three seasons. Since he was still only thirty-one, there was every reason to believe that more records were within his grasp, but they wouldn't be made in Milwaukee. For the end of the 1965 season was the end of another era for the peripatetic Braves. They had started in Boston. Now, after thirteen years in Milwaukee, they were headed for Atlanta.

So were the Aarons. The chance to have their son Larry with them all the year round was the dominant factor in their decision to move back to the South. They hated to leave Milwaukee, but with the ball club in Atlanta, their future was there.

12 The Atlanta Braves

HENRY AARON moved his family to Atlanta when the ball club moved. Having Larry home was the clinching argument, but there were other compensations, too. The Aarons were going into an upper-class integrated section of the most liberal city in the South. They had a spacious brick ranch house on two acres of grass. They were living where, as Barbara Aaron put it, "food prices are high and racial tensions low." And they were near both her people and Henry's.

In Atlanta, Henry was able to help the Braves become the first team to hire a Negro in a responsible front-office job. His brother-in-law, Barbara's brother, Bill Lucas, was a recent college graduate who wanted to get into baseball administration. Through Henry, he was hired as the club's assistant public relations director, but after that, he was on his own. He was later promoted to assistant farm director, where he did so well that his future was assured.

Now an established superstar, Aaron, who turned thirty-two in February, 1966, collected a salary in excess of $75,000 a year and was worth every cent of it. As always, he kept himself in good shape during the winter and this time was in perfect physical condition when he reported for spring training at West Palm Beach.

Bobby Bragan, the Braves manager, unhappy over the 1965 finish, was determined to take advantage of what speed the club had in 1966. This really meant mostly Aaron.

"In Aaron we have one of the five fastest men in the National League," Bragan told an observer in Florida. "This man could steal one-hundred bases a year if he wanted to. And we think we have others with good speed. There's no reason we couldn't become an effective hit-and-run club if we worked on it."

Bragan was upset that six 20-home-run hitters couldn't hoist the 1965 club higher than fifth, and he worried over just about everyone but Aaron. He knew Henry could be depended on to have a good year because Henry always had a good year. But there were defensive weaknesses in the infield, and the pitching staff was very shaky.

Unfortunately, Bragan couldn't make a silk purse out of a sow's ear. Henry Aaron, who averaged thirty-one steals a season, was fast, but most of his teammates were not. Furthermore, the pitching, which hadn't looked good on paper before the season began, looked worse after it started. The ball club got away to a miserable start and, despite another year of power hitting, didn't get any better until the last few weeks of the season.

The Atlanta debut was an unhappy one for everyone. On April 12, 1966, before more than 50,000 fans in the new stadium, the Braves lost a thirteen-inning game to the Pittsburgh Pirates, one of the preseason favorites to win the pennant. That in itself would not have been so bad, but the game was lost in the thirteenth on errors, the kinds of errors that cost ball games and drive managers out of their minds. The Braves infield was like a sieve—too much went through it. Almost from the beginning, Bragan had to experiment with it. Aaron's start was nearly as bad as the ball club's. In the long opening game he had one single in six trips to the plate. The next day, as the Pirates shut the Braves out, Aaron had no hits in four trips, so for his first two games of the year he went one for ten.

The club flew to New York for a series with the Mets, who had always been patsies for them. Aaron had a hit and drove in a run as the Braves won the first game, but they lost the next two to drop the series. In the three games Henry had a single and a double in 11 times at bat. In Philadelphia the next day he was hitless in four trips, but the Braves won.

Now the new Atlanta club had lost four games out of six, their ace slugger was barely over the .100 mark, his only extra-base hit a double against the Mets. Everyone, including the Phillies, knew it wouldn't last. Aaron would find his groove, and when he did, all baseball would know it. He found it more quickly than anyone expected—and in a most spectacular manner.

The Braves were in Philadelphia for the second game of their April series when Henry came to bat in the first inning with two out and a man on first. Ray Culp, the Phillies' pitcher, tried working around him, then threw a fast ball. Aaron, who had not been swinging well, came around perfectly and belted it into the left-field stands for a two-run homer.

That was his first of the 1966 season and the 399th of his career. And since the Phillies scored only one run in the game, that one swing of Aaron's was enough to clinch the ball game.

But he wasn't through. Later in the game he walked and flied out, then came up against Bo Belinsky in the first half of the ninth. Belinsky was as careful as Culp had been, but eventually he came in with the fast ball Aaron was looking for. Once again the wrists snapped, the bat came around and the ball disappeared into the left-field stands. And that second homer of the day was Aaron's 400th.

That clout gave Henry Aaron the distinction of becoming just the eleventh man in the history of baseball to hit 400 home runs. Ahead of him among the game's active players were only Willie Mays, Mickey Mantle and Henry's own heavy-hitting teammate, Eddie Mathews. None had reached the mark at as young an age as Aaron.

With this milestone behind him, he could look ahead to the 500 mark and perhaps beyond it. He had hit his last 100 homers in three years. If he could keep up the pace, he could conceivably hit 600, although Babe Ruth's record of 714 was beyond reach.

Asked about it, Henry simply shrugged in typical Aaron style and said, "I'm happy with four hundred. I never thought I'd hit this many."

Neither did anyone else when Aaron first broke into the majors. In those days he had been a hitter for average, not for power. Only after a couple of years did it become obvious that he could be a home-run hitter if he wanted to. In the early part of his career the homers came in the natural course of events. As the years passed, he worked harder and harder to pull the ball, trying to hit it in his power alley as all home-run hitters do.

By 1966 he had become a strong pull hitter without actually changing his wonderfully smooth stroke. Now he often knew when he could hit his pitch out of the park. He probably didn't actually try to hit any of his first 100 home runs, which were all accidents. It was only later in his career that he deliberately tried to hit home runs.

Even after he became a full-fledged pull hitter, he could go to center and right fields and often did. Still, some teams found it paid to shift on him, although nobody packed the left side of the diamond. The Pirates came closest. By 1966 they were playing him as a pull hitter, even going so far as to play Bill Mazeroski, their second baseman, behind the bag rather than in the normal second-base slot.

When they first tried it, someone asked Aaron if he would deliberately hit to right to break up the shift.

"Not normally," he added. "If I get my pitch, I'll

hit it to left. But if I don't, and it's in the strike zone, I'll go to right or right center."

He liked Atlanta much better than he expected to. The people of the city embraced him as an instant sports idol, and he found living there as pleasant as Milwaukee had been. Accommodating and friendly, he continued to be one of the easiest interviews in baseball, and he didn't care if the writers who approached him were from magazines, metropolitan newspapers, small-town papers, or high school weeklies. He treated everyone alike, with courtesy and the ever-present touch of gentle humor.

One day, before a game in Atlanta against the Giants, two youngsters from a local school approached him.

"Do you think a person can be an all-American in two sports?" one said.

"It's hard enough learning one," Aaron replied.

"Don't you like football?"

"From a safe distance."

"They're going to give Eddie Mathews a night," one of the boys said. "Have you ever had a night?"

"Son," Aaron said, "I have my night every game I get a base hit."

"Marichal is pitching tonight," the other boy said. "Do you think he can be hit?"

"Somebody's hitting him," Aaron said. "He's lost six games."

"Doesn't he scare you?"

Aaron grinned, held his bat out, moved it back and forth, then said, "Not as long as they let me swing this thing, son."

He still looked much the same as he had when he broke into baseball at eighteen, a circumstance which restaurant help sometimes found confusing. One day when he ordered a beer, the only alcoholic beverage he ever touched, the waitress said, "May I see your ID card?"

While Aaron broke up completely, one of the others with him said, "Why, that man is over thirty."

When Johnny McHale, the Braves' president, heard the story, he said to Henry, "Don't ever get older than thirty."

Judging by his play in 1966, Aaron was getting younger. Once he passed the 400 barrier in home runs, he clicked them off faster than anyone in the National League. One day he hit a home run off Ron Perranoski of the Dodgers which went like a shot into the center-field bleachers. It was his 13th hit in 16 tries against the Los Angeles relief pitcher.

"That man," Perranoski said, "ruins my earned run average. He remembers every pitch I ever threw him, no matter how I mix them up. And he always knows what to expect."

Even Sandy Koufax had his troubles with Aaron.

"He's the toughest in the league," Koufax said. "Just Bad Henry. There's no way you can pitch him when he's hot."

By the All-Star Game, although he was hitting only .280, Aaron had 26 homers, the most of his career at the halfway point of the season. It put him far ahead of everyone in homers. He also led in runs batted in, the other most significant slugging department.

But the ball club was going sour. Nothing that

Bragan did turned out right. The harassed Braves manager tried everything—probably too much. He seldom used the same infield two days in a row, and he constantly shuffled his batting order. If he had been getting results, nobody would have minded, but the combination of everlasting shifting around and consistent losing was too much. The ballplayers resented him, especially because of his treatment of Eddie Mathews. For some reason, Bragan went completely cold on the veteran slugger, who spent most of the first two-thirds of the season on the bench.

On August 9, with the club in eighth place and obviously going nowhere, Bragan was replaced as manager by Billy Hitchcock, one of his coaches. A former Baltimore manager, Hitchcock immediately began the tough job of rebuilding morale. His first move was to put Mathews back on third base with assurance that he would stay there, no matter what he hit. Hitchcock then set his lineup and batting order and sat back to watch the results.

They were excellent. Mathews responded by hitting a game-winning home run off a left-handed pitcher the first night he played. The club settled down and began going about the business of winning ball games. And for the rest of the season, the Braves didn't look like the same team.

They had much too far to go to get into the pennant race, but they moved up so fast that for a time they actually seemed dangerous. On August 31 they were in seventh place, four behind the sixth-place Reds and apparently anchored. But then they won four in a row, and after losing the first game of a doubleheader in

Pittsburgh on September 5, they rambled off on an eight-game winning streak.

Aaron helped win the first with his 37th homer, a two-run blast that provided the difference as the Braves beat the Pirates, 7–5. The next day Henry was hitless as the Braves won again, but on September 7, when the Braves won their third straight at Pittsburgh, Aaron broke loose with a double, three singles, two runs batted in, and a stolen base.

By then the Braves were at the .500 mark in wins and losses for the first time since May and tied with the slipping Reds for sixth place. It would take a miracle for them to overhaul the leading Dodgers, but they made a magnificent try, considering how low they were when the last month of the season began.

From Pittsburgh they went to New York, where they beat the Mets but lost Aaron for a day. Late in the game he pulled a leg muscle badly enough to force him out of action. He sat on the bench and watched the Braves win their fifth straight, but he insisted on getting back into the lineup for the last game of the Mets series on September 11.

Despite his bad leg—it bothered him for the rest of the season—Henry had a double and a single and batted in a run as the Braves swept the last of their three games in New York to run their winning streak to six.

They went on to Chicago where, after an off day, they exploded, crushing the Cubs, 10–2. Aaron led the attack, sparking a four-run first inning with one homer and belting another later in the game. On the fourteenth of the month he had two hits and another run batted in to lead the Braves to their eighth in a row.

That victory put them into a fifth-place tie with the Cardinals, 10½ games off the top and 2½ behind the fourth-place Phillies. But the Cubs stopped them the next day, and that slowed their drive for a higher place in the standings.

Still, they struggled into fourth place on September 21, when they passed the Phillies. On that date they were 4½ behind third place, 5 behind second, and 9½ behind the Dodgers. That was as close as they got, however. They slipped back into fifth place the last week of the season and finished there.

But they had given not only Atlanta fans, but National League followers everywhere a real run for the money. Nobody expected the Braves to finish in the first division at all, let alone 8 games over the .500 mark. Nor did anyone expect them to finish within 10 games of the pennant winner.

"If we could only have started sooner . . ."

It was the same old story. The season just didn't last long enough. The Braves had fallen into an unhappy pattern of getting off to a terrible start and playing catch-up for the rest of the year.

As usual, they were the heaviest hitting team in the league. Aaron led the way with 44 homers and 127 runs batted in, topping the league in both departments. Joe Torre hit 36 homers, Rico Carty 31, and Mack Jones 23, while Felipe Alou was beaten out for the batting championship only by his younger brother, Matty, of the Pirates.

Although Aaron batted .279, his lowest since coming to the big leagues, it was a most satisfying year for him. Among other things, he played in 158 games despite the crippling leg injury he suffered in September.

"Anybody else would have been through for the season," Hitchcock said. "But Henry never quits until he's a hospital case. Why, he even stole a couple of bases with that bad leg."

Hitchcock, a great admirer of Aaron's for years, gave the veteran slugger his head on the bases. Every time Aaron tried to steal, it was on his own. The fact that he was thrown out only three times in 24 attempts was a tribute to his judgment.

At the end of the 1966 season his lifetime home-run total was 442, putting him in tenth place on the all-time list of sluggers and within fairly easy reach of the 500 mark, considering his age and physical condition. He also set a National League record by coming to bat 603 times, his eighth year over 600. This mark was also reached by Vada Pinson of the Reds.

Where the Braves were going in the future remained to be seen. Two important front-office changes came just before the season ended. Paul Richards, a precise, intelligent baseball man, was named vice-president in charge of player personnel, obviously slated to become general manager. And Jim Fanning replaced the recently resigned John Mullen as farm director.

This meant little to Aaron. After his great season, he was sure to get another big raise, perhaps over the $100,000 figure, no matter whom he dealt with. Whatever he collected, nobody would begrudge him a cent. There wasn't a better all-around player in baseball.

13 Chieftan of the Braves

A month after the 1966 season ended, Henry went on a good will tour to South Vietnam with his teammate Joe Torre, Harmon Killebrew of the Minnesota Twins, and several other prominent sports figures. American servicemen on active duty had requested Aaron as one of their half-dozen favorite athletes. The trip lasted seventeen days, during which the athletes visited every combat area, living with and entertaining GI's wherever they went.

"It wasn't an easy trip," a spokesman for the group said later. "The living was primitive, the traveling dangerous, and the boys were under fire several times. There wasn't any question who the most sought-after athlete was. Everyone wanted to meet Henry Aaron."

On his return from the Orient Henry signed a two-year contract at a salary reported to be $100,000 a season. It was the first time the Braves had ever signed a ballplayer for more than one year.

"We want Henry to be satisfied," said William C. Bartholomay, the Braves' president. "He's been a superstar for a long time, and he deserves a superstar's contract."

Bartholomay didn't say so, but it was apparent that the real reason for the two-year pact was to assure Aaron that he would not be traded. In a rash moment Paul Richards, by then the general manager, had announced that there were no untouchables on the ball club. When asked if that meant even Aaron might be trade bait, he had said it meant anyone might be trade bait. Since he could not retract the statement without looking foolish, and Bartholomay couldn't contradict him, Aaron's long-term contract was the only solution to what could have become a touchy problem.

While the salary was comparable to top salaries everywhere in baseball, there was no doubt that Aaron would have been better off elsewhere financially. He had spent his entire big-league career in Milwaukee and Atlanta, where outside opportunities for ballplayers to make money are comparatively few.

"If he had played in New York, Chicago, Los Angeles, San Francisco, or Boston, he'd have made a fortune," a baseball observer remarked. "But he could never make much more than his salary in the towns where the Braves were."

Asked how he felt about the situation, Aaron smiled and said, "I've been happy. The Braves have treated me well."

"But what if you had played in New York?" someone said.

"If I had played in New York," Aaron said calmly, "I believe I would have made two million dollars."

Another time he showed mild annoyance when an observer asked him why he had never given fans or writers anything special to look for in him.

"Why, outside of 'Hank,' which your friends rarely use, you don't even have a nickname," the observer said. "You don't give anyone a chance to think of you as anything but a ballplayer."

"That's all I want to be," Aaron said. "I was never a 'Say Hey' kid, never one of the M and M boys, my cap never fell off when I ran for a fly ball, and I never did anything special."

His references were to Willie Mays, the "Say Hey" kid, and to Roger Maris and Mickey Mantle, who became the M and M boys when Maris hit 61 homers and Mantle 54 for the Yankees in 1961. Aaron didn't bother to point out that he and Eddie Mathews were far ahead of Mantle and Maris in total homers.

Mathews, Aaron's last link with the past, left the Braves without fanfare or, for that matter, even an announcement, when he was traded to the Houston Astros in December. The story broke out of Houston, and the first Mathews heard about it was when a newspaperman called him for a statement. This caused considerable resentment on the part of Mathews' admirers, for it was indeed a crudely abrupt ending for a player who had been with the Braves as long as he.

Aaron's only reaction was tinged with the sadness that comes on the departure of an old colleague.

"I'll miss him," Henry said. "He's a great guy and a great friend and was always a wonderful teammate."

Manager Billy Hitchcock had high hopes for his ball club when he met it at spring training—and the principal reason was Aaron. Henry started as if he had never stopped, hitting the ball hard right from the first day. He climaxed a magnificent spring training with two home runs in an exhibition game with the Twins in Atlanta.

Later Aaron was asked why he worked so hard in exhibition games, which, after all, didn't mean anything.

"When I put on this uniform, I'm all business," Aaron said. "That's the only way. If you don't go all out even in exhibition games, you tend to get complacent. I don't want that."

After the game with the Twins, Aaron flew to Washington for one of the most thrilling experiences of his life. With Torre, Killibrew, Baseball Commissioner William D. Eckert, and the two major-league presidents, Warren Giles and Joe Cronin, he was invited to the White House by President Lyndon B. Johnson. There the President asked the ballplayers questions about their South Vietnam trip, addressing several directly to Aaron.

Later Henry told a friend, "Imagine me, a poor kid from Mobile, meeting the President of the United States in the White House!"

The Braves opened the season at the Astrodome

in Houston. Thanks to their old pal Mathews, they got off on the wrong foot. He belted a triple to drive in the tying and winning runs on opening day, then helped the Astros win the next two games. The Braves won their next five, but after that, they were up and down, mostly down, because they couldn't get rolling.

Aaron, meanwhile, appeared to be off on his greatest season. For the first few weeks he couldn't do any wrong. He got a hit or two almost every day, although it took him two weeks to get his first homer.

When he did, off Dave Giusti of the Astros at Atlanta, he matched it with a second before the game was over. They were the 443rd and 444th of his career. He was zeroing in on the magic 500 mark.

After that Astro game, Giusti said, "From now on, that guy will never see anything from me but curves and sliders."

Aaron laughed when told of Giusti's remark.

"That will suit me fine. Giusti has a real good fast ball. I can't hit it when he gets it where he wants it. He didn't today."

By mid-May Aaron was leading the league in homers, runs batted in, and runs. He was third in batting and fourth in hits, but the ball club still wasn't going anywhere. The Braves were playing just about .500 ball and could not struggle out of fifth place, though they weren't far behind the leaders.

One day Aaron wrecked Juan Marichal and the Giants all by himself. Besides getting four hits in five times up, he actually stole the game. After stealing twice in the first nine innings, he singled in the tenth, stole second, and scored the winning run on an error.

"That man!" said Marichal after the game. "If he doesn't beat you one way, he beats you another."

In the 11 games the Braves played between June 1 and June 14, Aaron batted .500 with 23 hits in 46 times up. He hit safely in every game and upped his batting average to .335, but the Braves couldn't get out of fifth place.

In mid-June Aaron was a definite threat for the Triple Crown, since he led the league in home runs, was fourth in runs batted in and fifth in batting. In the meantime, he continued to move up in the all-time individual standings, chipping away at records here and there, passing one milestone after another.

On June 27, Aaron hit the 11th grand-slam homer of his career, breaking a tie with Ernie Banks of the Cubs for leadership among the active players. When told that the all-time grand-slam leader was Lou Gehrig with 23, Aaron said, "I guess that's one record I can forget."

After the season's All-Star Game, the Braves' fortunes picked up, as if everyone on the ball club had decided it was time to try as hard as Aaron did. With the higher ranking teams in close range of one another, they had a good shot at the top. Ahead of them were the Cardinals, the Cubs, the Giants, and the Reds in that order, but first-place St. Louis outpaced Atlanta by only seven games.

A four-game winning streak moved the Braves up into fourth place as the Giants slipped behind them. When they went into St. Louis for a weekend series they were only four and one-half games back of the Cardinals. They won the first game, to go three and one-half behind, and it appeared they were really going to make a run for the roses.

Then the roof fell in. They dropped a Sunday doubleheader to slip five and one-half behind first place, and they never recovered. Although for a couple of weeks they were in third place, trailing only the Cardinals and the Cubs, they kept falling behind in games. Once they had lost that weekend chance in St. Louis, they were dead.

On July 31, Aaron hit a home run off Curt Simmons of the Cubs, his 27th of the season and the 469th of his career. More important, it was his 1,500th run batted in, prompting an observer to write, "It seems every time Henry Aaron swings his bat he breaks a record."

"Setting records," he replied, "only means you're getting old."

But he was pleased just the same, for every record, no matter how obscure, meant something to him. Asked what goals he had left, he responded, "The one thing I really want to do is get three thousand hits. Then everything else will fall into place—the home runs, the runs batted in, everything. But you have to hit the ball before you can set the records."

By September, Aaron's records were the only interesting things about the Braves. The close of the season witnessed a tight contest between Aaron and Jim Wynn of the Astros for the player with the most home runs. Aaron finally came out on top with 39. His 113 runs scored equalled Lou Brock's achievement that year, and his 37 doubles left him second only to Rusty Staub of the Astros.

Aaron was a very close third in RBI's, finishing two behind Clemente, the leader, and one behind Orlando Cepeda of the Cardinals, who was second. Henry was also fifth in hits and eighth in batting, with a .307 mark.

His long-term records came in bunches. During that 1967 season he went beyond his 2,000th game, his 1,600th single, his 1,500th run, his 1,000th extra-base hit, his 4,500th total base, his 2,600th hit, and his 1,500th RBI. When he scored more than 100 runs for the thirteenth straight year, he went into a tie with Vada Pinson for the all-time lead.

By the end of the season Aaron held eleven Braves batting records and two National League records and was threatening some of the home run citadels. Considering his age and condition, there seemed almost no limit to where he might go.

His 37 homers gave him a career total of 481 in fourteen years. This was less time than it had taken any of the others ahead of him to reach their totals. Lou Gehrig hit 493 homers in seventeen years; Eddie Mathews, 509 in sixteen; Mel Ott, 511 in sixteen; Mickey Mantle, 518 in seventeen; Ted Williams, 521 in twenty-two; Jimmy Foxx, 534 in twenty-one, and Willie Mays, 564 in seventeen. Through 1967 Aaron had been hitting home runs at the rate of 100 every three years. If he could maintain his pace for three years, he would probably pass everyone but Ruth.

But Ruth's record?

"I'll never make it," Henry said.

His Braves finished in seventh place, four games below the .500 mark. Henry criticized his teammates by saying, "We have too many guys talking about hunting and fishing and golf and outside business interests. You can't win baseball games without concentrating on baseball."

The Braves' poor showing forced the firing of manager Hitchcock three days before the end of the season. He was later replaced by a friend of Paul Richards, Luman Harris.

Harris would manage the Braves in their 1969 season—truly their most joyous since 1957. For the first time, the Atlanta franchise was part of the new National League West which also included the Reds, the Astros, the Dodgers, the Padres and the Giants. The Braves, led by outfielder Rico Carty, closed the season with a 17-victory-and-3-loss drive propelling them into the playoffs with Cincinnati.

The Reds led 2-1 in the contest until the seventh inning when Luman Harris substituted two pinch hitters. Reds pitcher Wayne Granger then walked Aaron to load the bases. Carty sacrificed a fly to right field to drive in the winning run. Centerfielder Gonzalez had hit his fourth single of the day earlier in the inning to tie the score. Good pitching retired all Reds except Jim Stewart who hit a deep fly to right center where it was caught by Aaron.

After the game frenzied fans raced onto the field, pulling up bases for souvenirs while the ballplayers drank champagne and toasted to victory in the pennant championship.

In the early spring of 1969 a few of the foolhardy bet on the Mets' vying for the National League Pennant with odds of 100-to-1 against them. Yet the first weekend of an Indian summer October saw the improbable Mets pitted against the Braves. Having won one hundred games in the season as well as the Eastern Divisional title, the cocky Mets went south prepared to meet the Braves.

As the teams confronted each other, they posed a classically simple question—could good pitching hold good hitting at bay? Could the Mets' Tom Seaver and Jerry Koosman stop Henry Aaron, Orlando Cepeda and Rico Carty?

Aaron himself gave his estimation of Mets' pitching strength. "Their pitching compares with the Dodgers when they had Koufax and Drysdale. Koosman and Seaver are the closest to those two."

The Mets entered the eighth inning of the first game behind the Braves by a single run, 5-4. Wayne Garret hit a ground ball just inside the third base line and was sent home to tie the game by a pop-fly hit by Cleon Jones. Jones scored by stealing third and crossing the plate on a wild throw by Cepeda. J. C. Martin was substituted for Seaver in the line-up and hit a single with the bases loaded. Toni Gonzalez let the ball get by him, so that two more runs scored, but recovered the ball in time to force Martin out at third. The Mets took the first game in the series by

9-5 and forced oddsmakers to favor them for the remaining games.

A puzzled and disappointed Aaron declared, "It was the hardest we ever hit Seaver. When you score five runs off Seaver, you beat him. Well, you think you're going to win."

Aaron scored a double and a homer off Seaver. Discussing his pitching, Aaron offered clues about his approach at the plate.

"He made a few mistakes. I was guessing both times I hit the ball—I guessed in the seventh that he'd throw a curve. He did both times. If he'd thrown a fastball on the home run, I'd probably have struck out."

The other great pitching star of the Mets, Jerry Koosman, played the second game of the series. He, too, made grave mistakes, as had Seaver the day before. In the fifth inning, with two out, the Mets were leading 9-1. But the precision and agility of Henry Aaron closed the gap sufficiently to force Mets manager Gil Hodges to remove Koosman. Henry hit a three-run homer and was followed by Clete Boyer's hitting a two-run single. The score was 9-5.

Unfortunately the Braves' pitchers were little better, as is shown in the final score, 11-6. Luman Harris found it inexplicable. He started with Ron Reed, who had beaten the Mets twice during the year, giving up four runs in twenty-eight innings. Now he gave up this many in two.

Harris sounded a genuine note of despair after the loss of the second game.

"We've got one foot in the grave and we've got to get up and play baseball or get beat. . . . I don't understand why our pitchers are so damn wild. It's unbelievable. . . ."

The teams shifted to New York for the third game where a victory for the Mets would give them the National League championship and, of course, send them on to the Series. Gary Gentry was the Mets starting pitcher and in the first inning gave up a single to Gonzalez whom "Hammerin' Henry" sent home on a 410-foot drive that rebounded off the center field flag pole. The Mets were hitting equally well and scored twice to tie the game.

The third inning saw the top of Atlanta's batting order again with Gonzalez singling and Aaron following him with a double. The Mets changed pitchers, going with Jim Ryan. Their fortunes shifted considerably and they were able to dispose of this third inning threat. The bottom of the third saw the Mets score, moving into the lead. In the fifth, Atlanta scored two more runs, only to be held at bay with a Mets rally for two runs, putting them ahead 5-4. With Ryan's excellent pitching in the remaining innings, the Braves scored no more while the Mets drove in two more, winning the game 7-4 and taking the series.

The Braves were surely upset at the loss but the ebullience of the Mets carried the day. Against those 100 to 1 odds, the amazing Mets had won the National League Championship.

The close of this disappointing 1969 season saw Henry Aaron draw closer to that goal he had set for

Chieftan of the Braves

himself—to have three thousand hits. A month into the next season the Atlanta slugger accomplished it.

The occasion elicited this comment from one New York sports writer: "The first name listed in the Baseball Register, a compilation of 10,000 men who have played major league ball in the last century, is Henry Aaron. That is most appropriate since he is close to the top of many statistical lists measuring baseball greatness. On May 17th in his seventeenth year of playing, he hit three thousand hits. Only eight others have done this."

Bobby Bragan, a former manager of the Braves, said, "If you need a base, he'll steal it quietly. If you need a shoestring catch, he'll make it and his hat won't fly off and he won't fall . . . ."

Paul Richards, Henry's general manager, acknowledged his accomplishments and recalled that his importance cannot be seen in the figures alone. "Statistics actually hide his value to our club. More than anything else, he's a game winner."

From Mickey Mantle came this praise: "As far as I'm concerned, Aaron is the best player of my era. He is to baseball of the last fifteen years what Joe di Maggio was before him."

14 The Magic Number

By age thirty-four Henry Aaron was the oldest, most experienced of all the Braves, an elder statesman who could calmly look far back and make an accurate appraisal of himself. He was, in fact, at peace with the world and used the opportunity to reflect.

"I'm more mellow than I used to be," he told an Atlanta writer. "Maybe that's why trophies and honors and prizes mean more to me than they used to." He sat in his living room, put his feet up and said, "Whenever I sit here in this wonderful room with the people and things I love all around me, I remember where I came from. Life was tough for me as a kid. It makes me appreciate what I have today."

He was a $100,000 ball player now, but he lived by standards he had been taught growing up. "I don't throw money around," he said. "I can remember when it was so terribly hard to come by. I've got a nice home, but I can get along without too much show." He was not typical of most big-league hitters of whom Ralph Kiner once said, "Home-run hitters drive Cadillacs." Henry Aaron did nothing of the sort.

By 1970 he had signed a two-year contract guaranteeing him $200,000 a year, and while the salary was most gratifying, it was not because of how much it could buy. "You can use only so much money. Beyond that how much do you really need? You can take pride in the fact that you can command as a Mays or a Mantle, because that means you're in the same class with them. They're superstars, and it's nice to know that you're considered a superstar, too." For Henry Aaron this was a statement of unusual boasting, but considering what the next years held for him, it was characteristically understated.

After Aaron closed his seventh season in Atlanta in 1971, he modestly reversed his earlier statement that he would never hit 714 runs by admitting, "I began to think for the first time that I had a shot at the Babe's record." In the years since he had come to Atlanta, Aaron had successive totals of 44, 39, 29, 44, 38, 47. Thus, when the '72 season registered 34, it was indeed time for the countdown to begin.

But as it did, the pressure mounted. Comparisons with Ruth would have to be sustained. Not the least of them was one offered by a computer late in the 1973 season. It pronounced, "Babe Ruth's record of 714 home runs won't be broken by Hank Aaron until

September 30th at the earliest." It called odds three-to-one against his breaking the mark at all that season, but one of its programmers said:

"One factor we can't measure is whether the pitchers are making it harder for him to connect. Another is the emotional factor." Circumstances made that last factor a most trying one.

As his fame grew and as he charged Ruth's record, there grew the ugly and frightful specter of racism. In 1973 he was receiving 600 letters a day, most of them complimenting him and urging him on to greater fame. But a disturbing number expressed racial hatred—and none was signed, of course. Aaron said, "Some people seem to feel I'm getting into an area where no black man has the right to be. . . . I can't believe in this kind of resentment."

In the same season racist slurs from fans in Atlanta angered the imperturbable Aaron and elicited a clenched fist of defiance. Henry spoke of the sorrow indicated by his gesture:

"It's worse because it's happening in my own ball park, in front of people I've played for in hundreds of games. I try to pass it off as ignorance. I know it happens all over the world, but I'm concerned about Atlanta."

All this must have proved most dismaying to a man who only the winter before had organized a bowling tournament which raised $25,000 for the treatment and research of sickle cell anemia, a disease common among blacks.

Heartening, though, was the infrequency of occurrences such as that dreadful game. The overriding majority of letters supported him. The applause from fans both black and white was warm each time he moved closer to 714.

Did Aaron feel pressure from the quest itself? This was certainly the question most frequently asked him by reporters.

He said, "It was different with Roger Maris (who broke Ruth's season record of 60 home runs). He was under time pressure, and I'm not. I've got all the time in the world, and if I don't do it this season, I'll do it next season. But I know that unless I get hit by a truck, I'll do it."

While all these conflicts were reported in the papers, it is likely they reflect the tensions of the public rather than those of the confident ball player. When Aaron finally hit the crucial home run, he did so before the tension mounted, almost before the scene was set. His hitting of number 714 perfectly symbolizes his prowess and control.

On the first day of the new season with the first swing of the bat, Henry Aaron put a four hundred foot line drive over the left center field fence of Cincinnati's Riverside Stadium. It brought in two additional runs by sending Ralph Garr and Michael Lum home. Lum ran halfway to second base when he heard the crack of the bat and started to talk to the ball.

"Get up! Get up!"

It did.

The Braves' dugout was silent as the ball climbed and sped farther and farther away.

Did the hitter watch the ball?

"Nope," said Henry, "I never do. That's the umpire's job. Let him do it."

The Cincinnati pitcher, right-hander Jack Billingham described his delivery: "The ball was slippery. It was going toward the outside part of the plate and it tailed in. It was my mistake. But that's what makes Henry Aaron great. He hits mistakes. When I went out there, my main thought was not to let him beat me. He almost did. He's great."

For eight innings it looked as if Billingham's fears would be realized as the Braves accumulated a 6-2 lead. But the "Red Machine" diminished the difference with homers by Dave Concepcion, Tony Perez and finally Pete Rose, who tied it in the ninth with a single driving a runner in. In the eleventh, Rose hit, advanced to second, and on a wild throw by Buzz Capra, scored to win the game. The fifty-two thousand Cincinnati fans went home delighted, having seen Aaron in such a historic moment and a Reds victory.

Aaron didn't celebrate. The Braves didn't win.

Aaron's father, brother and second wife, whom he married only four and a half months earlier following his divorce, attended. Mrs. Billye Williams Aaron, an Atlanta talk show personality who has been active in the civil rights movement, was interviewed.

"Did you notice any change in Henry Aaron lately—any tension or irritability?"

"No, none at all. You've been writing sports

articles for a long time and should know Henry is Henry and he doesn't change. He doesn't bring his job home with him.

"You know I don't know why everyone is interviewing me. I never hit a home run in my life. . . . I am on leave from my job at WSB until Henry hits number 715. That means I'll be back at work soon."

Four days later the Braves were back in Atlanta to play the Los Angeles Dodgers. Fifty-three thousand fans jammed the stadium while millions watched on television.

Aaron was fourth in the line-up, and came to bat in the second inning. He never swung. Dodger pitcher Al Downing walked him. Dusty Baker hit a double and Aaron scored. He returned to the Braves' dugout to study the pitcher's habits, as he always does.

"I started thinking about Al Downing of the Dodgers on the way home from Cincinnati. Basically, I knew what he would like me to hit—his fastball, which tails away and, if he's right, is his best pitch. I knew he didn't want to throw me curve balls, which from a lefthander would come inside and which I could pull. So I mentally set myself for that one pitch I knew he'd rely on—his fastball. I can discipline myself to wait for that ball. I knew it would come sooner or later."

It did, in the fourth inning. Atlanta was trailing at that point, 3-1. Two men were on base when Aaron came to bat. Downing pitched one ball, inside.

Then, on his next pitch, Downing made his

momentous mistake. It was a high fastball—which Aaron had disciplined himself to wait for. Aaron lashed his bat like a whip. And Babe Ruth's record number of home runs became a matter of baseball history.

Aaron continued to act like himself, saying, "I feel I can relax now. I feel my team-mates can relax. I feel I can have a great season."

How many more he hit did not matter much. He had broken the record.

But can another player in the future beat Aaron's record?

Back in 1967, when he had been asked if he could beat Ruth's record, Aaron had replied, "I'll never make it."

That remark showed it's never safe to prophesy about baseball. As Henry Aaron demonstrated, the one sure thing about baseball is that no one can say what will happen next in that fascinating game.

Index

Aaron, Barbara Lucas, 42–43, 64, 79–80, 142, 153
Aaron, Billye Williams, 183, 184
Aaron, Henry, *See* specific names, subjects
Aaron, Herbert and Estelle, 19 ff., 183
Aaron, Tommie, 126 ff., 131, 143
Adair, Bill, 31, 34–35
Adcock, Joe, 9, 12, 45, 73, 77, 95–96, 107–8, 118 ff., 124, 129
Alabama, 19 ff., 79–80
All-Star Games, 60, 62–63, 78, 135
Alou, Felipe, 142 ff.
Alston, Walter, 61, 132–33
Antonelli, Johnny, 75–76
Astros, 169, 173
Atlanta, 8, 139 ff., 153 ff., 166, 181

Baker, Gene, 35, 36
Bartholomay, William C., 166
Baserunning, 38, 52–53. *See also* Records
Bats, 40, 74
Batting style, 10–12, 15, 20–21, 27, 32 ff., 41–42, 44, 175, 184
Billingham, Jack, 183
Boners, 97, 107–8
Bragan, Bobby, 66–67, 75, 129, 143–44, 154–55, 177
Braves, 7 ff., 29–30, 31 ff. *See also* Pennant races; specific names
Bruton, Bill, 45, 73, 78, 89, 93, 95–96, 122, 126, 147
Bunting, 59
Burdette, Lew, 9, 12 ff., 45, 51–52, 73, 83 ff., 91, 94, 99, 106, 110 ff., 120, 129
Business enterprises, 147, 179–80

Cardinals, 7, 12 ff., 51, 64–65, 68–69, 76, 101, 145, 170 ff. *See also* Pennant races; specific names
Carty, Rico 143, 146, 173, 174

Catchers, 10
Center field, 9, 78, 122–23
Cepeda, Orlando, 174
Clemente, Roberto, 144, 152
Covington, Wes, 9, 12 ff., 78, 89, 95, 132
Crandall, Del, 9, 45, 73, 75, 78–79, 95–96, 129, 142
Cubs, 170

DiMaggio, Joe, 21, 64, 177
Discrimination and racism, 21, 25, 34, 37, 42, 79–80, 142, 153–54, 181
Dodgers, 8, 21, 24–25, 52, 57–58, 61, 67 ff., 73 ff., 80–81, 92, 109 ff., 118, 132–33, 173, 183. *See also* Pennant races; specific names
Downing, Al, 184
Dressen, Charlie, 10, 38, 116–117, 122, 124–25
Durocher, Leo, 30

Earnings, 24, 15, 29–30, 37, 61, 71–72, 89, 116–117, 122–23, 154, 179–80
Eau Claire (Wis.), 31–36
Expansion teams, 121

Family and youth, 19 ff.
Fines, 56–57, 124–25
Ford, Whitey, 95 ff.
Fox, Charlie, 32
Frick, Ford, 57
Friend, Bob, 58–59

Gehrig, Lou, 149–50, 170
Geraghty, Ben, 37–39
Giants, 27, 30, 75–76, 91–92, 94, 101, 105, 109 ff., 170–171, 173 *See also* Pennant races; specific names
Giusti, Dave, 169
Golden Gloves, 135

187

Griggs, Dewey, 26, 28, 29–30
Grimm, Charlie, 12, 45, 47–48, 50, 52, 57, 59, 62

Haddix, Harvey, 106–8
Haney, Fred, 12, 17–18, 38, 62, 71–72, 78–79, 90 ff., 94, 100, 107, 116
Harris, Luman, 173, 175
Hazle, Bob, 78
Hitchcock, Billy, 167, 173
Hitting, .400, 101 ff.; records, 173, 177. (*See also* Records); streaks, 63 ff., 91, 102 ff., 110, 127–28; 1000th hit, 109, 130; 2000th hit, 146; 3000th hit, 177.
Holmes, Tommy, 64–65
Home runs, 7. 16, 29, 51, 72, 74, 80 ff., 93, 109, 115, 119, 124, 125, 128 ff., 133 ff., 146, 149 ff., 169, 170–72, 176, 180, 182 ff., 185
Hornsby, Roger, 66, 103–4, 130
Humor, 39–40, 49, 59, 67, 106

Indianapolis Clowns, 25–30, 31, 32
Injuries and illness, 54–55, 72, 79, 90, 105, 127, 147–48, 151

Jacksonville Tars, 37–43
Johnson, Lyndon B., 160

Killebrew, Harmon, 165
Koosman, Jerry, 174–75
Koufax, Sandy, 174

Law, Vernon, 66–67
Left field, 49 ff.
Logan, Johnny, 9, 12 ff., 45, 60, 75, 78, 88, 95, 121, 123
Lucas, Bill, 153–54

Mantilla, Felix, 37, 78, 107–8
Mantle, Mickey, 167, 177
Marichal, Juan, 170
Maris, Roger, 167
Marriage and home life, 43, 79–80, 141–42, 147, 152, 183
Mathews, Eddie, 9, 12 ff., 45, 61, 73 ff., 85, 88, 95, 104, 109–10, 118, 119, 124, 131 ff., 146, 149–50, 167–68, 169.
Mays, Willie, 9, 30, 82, 93, 128, 167
Menke, Dennis, 143, 146.
Mets, 174 ff.
Milwaukee, 7 ff., 79–80, 86, 88–89, 92–93, 120–21, 124, 133, 138 ff., 147 ff.
Mobile, 19 ff., 79–80
Mobile Black Bears, 24–25
Moon, Wally, 13, 14, 66, 68
Most Valuable Player, 42, 55, 87, 135
Musial, Stan, 14–15, 21–23, 81, 82, 87, 93, 125, 146

National League West, 173
Negro American League, 25 ff.
Northern League, 31 ff.
Number, 50, 75

O'Connell, Danny, 45, 46, 60, 73, 76, 77
Outfield, 44, 46 ff., 60, 123, 135–36, 172, 186–87
Owen, Mickey, 43–44

Padres, 173
Pafko, Andy, 9, 12 ff., 45, 48, 73, 78, 83, 95
Pendleton, James, 35, 36, 46, 48, 49
Pennant races: 1956, 61 ff.; 1957, 7 ff., 12 ff., 73 ff.; 1958, 91 ff.; 1959, 100 ff.; 1960, 118–21; 1961, 124; 1964, 145 ff.; 1965, 148 ff.; 1969, 173 ff.
Perini, Lou, 61, 89
Perranoski, Ron, 135
Personality, 16–17, 23, 24, 28, 34, 39–40, 46 ff., 59–60, 65, 67, 106, 124, 136–37, 143, 167, 168, 179, 182
Phillies, 27, 145
Pirates, 58–59, 66–67, 74, 75, 106–8, 118. *See also* Pennant races; specific names
Pitchers, 10, 32–33, 40, 42, 46–47, 51–52, 58–59, 66–67, 73, 103, 106–8, 118–19, 132, 135, 151, 174–75.

Index

Play-offs, 112–115
Pollock, Syd, 25, 26, 29, 30
Pritchett Athletics, 24
Puerto Rican League, 43–44

Quinn, John, 35, 48, 61, 116

Raschi, Vic, 51
Records, 7, 21, 29, 35, 36, 42, 55, 60 ff., 72 ff., 78, 82 ff., 90 ff., 101 ff., 115, 119, 124–25, 127 ff., 146, 149 ff., 169–71, 177, 180, 182 ff. *See also* Pennant races
Reds, 50, 53–54, 68, 73 ff., 104, 170, 173, 182, *See also* Pennant races; specific names
Richards, Paul, 166, 177
Right field, 60, 123, 135
Roberts, Robin, 47, 102
Robinson, Jackie, 21, 25, 29
Rookie of the year, 36
Ruth, Babe, 149–50, 173, 180, 185

Schoendienst, Red, 9, 12 ff., 76 ff., 81, 83, 89, 93, 97, 100, 110, 117, 121
Seaver, Tom, 174–75
Second base, 40–41, 60, 117, 144
Shortstop, 26, 31 ff., 41
Signs, 39

Simmons, Curt, 11, 46–47
Slumps, 62, 74, 82, 90
Social work, 136–37, 181
South Atlantic League, 37 ff.
Southworth, Billy, 35–36
Spahn, Warren, 10, 45, 51–52, 68–69, 73, 83 ff., 94 ff., 110, 120, 129, 133, 144, 147
Spring training, 45 ff., 56 ff., 61, 71, 129–30, 148, 168
Stolen bases, 38

Tebbetts, Birdie, 116, 125, 126, 129
Television, 139–40, 141
Thomson, Bobby, 16, 45, 46, 48, 53–54, 73, 77
Torre, Frank, 77, 78, 95
Torre, Joe, 143–44, 146, 165
Toulminville (Ala.), 20 ff.
Triple Crown, 82–83, 131 ff., 170

Vietnam, 165

Waner, Paul, 90
World Series, 1957, 83–86; 1958, 93–99

Yankees, 27, 74–75, 83–86, 93–99. *See also* Pennant races; specific names

The Author

When Al Hirshberg died on April 11, 1973, American sports fans lost one of their most popular writers. Among his widely read books from Putnam's were *Frank Howard: The Gentle Giant; Baseball's Greatest Catchers; The Glory Runners.* None of his books has been more popular than *Henry Aaron: Quiet Superstar,* first published in 1969. Now a new writer, Mark Denton, has picked up the story where Hirshberg left it and tells how Henry Aaron became the new home run king.

Sports Shelf Biographies You Will Enjoy

VIDA BLUE:
Coming Up Again
by Don Kowet

TOM SEAVER OF THE METS
by George Sullivan

ERNIE BANKS:
Mr. Cub
by Bill Libby

TONY CONIGLIARO:
Up From Despair
by Robert Rubin

BABE RUTH:
His Story in Baseball
by Lee Allen

DIZZY DEAN
by Lee Allen

KEN BOYER
by David Lipman

LOU GEHRIG:
A Quiet Hero
by Frank Graham

MICKEY MANTLE:
Mr. Yankee
by Al Silverman

MY UPS AND DOWNS IN BASEBALL
by Orlando Cepeda
with Charles Einstein

ROBERTO CLEMENTE:
Batting King
by Arnold Hano

ROY CAMPANELLA:
A Man of Courage
by Gene Schoor

SANDY KOUFAX:
Strikeout King
by Arnold Hano

SATCHEL PAIGE:
All Time Baseball Great
by Robert Rubin

TED WILLIAMS
by Ray Robinson

WILLIE MAYS:
Coast to Coast Giant
by Charles Einstein

JOHNNY BENCH:
The Little General
by Bill Libby

PETE ROSE:
They Call Him "Charlie Hustle"
by Bill Libby

FRANK HOWARD:
The Gentle Giant
by Al Hirshberg

WILLIE STARGELL:
Baseball Slugger
by Bill Libby

BOSTON PUBLIC LIBRARY

No longer the property of the
Boston Public Library.
Sale of this material benefits the Library.

Boston Public Library

Copley Square

General Library

GV865
.A25H5
1974

1188459003

The Date Due Card in the pocket indicates the date on or before which this book should be returned to the Library. Please do not remove cards from this pocket.